# ADVANCE PRAISE FOR
## The Adventures of Silly Billy

## Sillogy: Volume 1.

*"The Adventures of Silly Billy are a must read for anyone that wants to return to their childhood and relive adventures similar to their own, or for those people that did not get to enjoy an adventurous childhood and would like to go along for the bike ride. Either way, the reader is in for a treat and that treat just might be a trip with Silly Billy and the Good Deed.*

*Greg McVicker skillfully tells his childhood adventures with vivid descriptions and heartfelt sincerity that you really do feel that you are right there beside him and experiencing the same adventures. You soon find yourself wondering what is going to happen to this loveable, yet accident prone young boy and I sure hope he gets out of this mishap without any harm or consequences. These stories will amuse as well as entertain when you see the world through the eyes of a child and the logic of Silly Billy in every one of his stories.*

*A wonderful read for anyone that wants to experience a simpler life and time as well as a side of the Belfast Child's life before his world is turned upside down with unforeseen realties."*

- Kristine Parkhurst Howser,
Cedar Rapids, Iowa, USA.

"Brilliant. Loved the book and the memories it brought back. It was lovely to read about Knockview and thank you for bringing back memories of the wonderful people we grew up with. We were very lucky to live where we did in such a terrible time in the history of Northern Ireland. We were known as the children of the troubles now we are the adults of peace. Greg, I still see some of the people you have written about and I am going to say to them about your book."

- Linda Donnelly (nee Stanley),
Knockview Road, Newtownabbey, Northern Ireland.


"The girls and I read the stories together. They had snacks and drinks while I read, and they laughed the whole time!

After we were done, Zoe was still laughing and said she thought it was all really funny and gave it a perfect 5 stars! Scarlet added she thought it was worth 8 stars out of 5 it was THAT good!

I thought it was fun to read it as a family while we shared in Silly Billy's adventures together!"

- Zoe Penner (age 13),
Scarlet Penner (age 11),
and Dale Doucette,
Winnipeg, Manitoba, Canada.

"I liked Silly Billy – his mistakes and adventures made me laugh and he tries so hard – he is just like me! We travelled to Ireland this year and I could imagine the streets and places that Billy lives. My family enjoyed reading this together and I think other families will too!"

"Enjoyed the book immensely! Lots of laughs and conversation about not giving up and learning from our mistakes. Billy teaches us to always try our best and not give up – wise words learned from a wee lad. Thanks for sharing your stories with us."

- Lauren (age 9) and Shannon Ivsek, Winnipeg, Manitoba, Canada.

"We liked the Silly Billy stories. Billy's adventures on Thunder made us cringe, and laugh! We especially like the Postage Stamp story. We were glad he finally finished his chore and was proud of himself! We liked the twist at the end!"

- Sam, Ethan and Jen Van Winkle, Winnipeg, Manitoba, Canada.

*"A new book from the Irish Author and Poet, Greg McVicker, is always something to look forward to and to enjoy. This latest offering does not disappoint. Magical for children and adults of any age!*

*Although Silly Billy saw the light of day several years ago, this trilogy brings three wonderful adventures of the hapless but kind Silly Billy. His tales of his boyhood around his hometown on the outskirts of Belfast, growing up in The Troubles but still enjoying his childhood.*

*This trilogy brings heartfelt laughter, then a sudden tear, not to mention how Silly Billy was appalled when his brother stole some money from their Da to pay for a day out at Carrickfergus Castle near 7 miles from their home.*

*Greg (aka Silly Billy) cleverly uses his family and school friend as his base for his childhood stories, entwining their characters, and he uses vivid descriptions of the surrounding streets and countryside near his childhood home. You laugh and cry with him as he takes us on the journey.*

*Although I live in the UK, I have been taken around some of Greg's childhood haunts with Greg as my guide, and can seem them clearly in my mind as I read his amazing stories.*

*Can't wait for the next book!"*

- Jean Camp
Plymouth, England, UK.

*"Silly Billy is a funny character that always is getting in trouble. His thoughts on his world around him always cracked me up! My only wish for this book was that the books were longer to get more of Silly Billy's silly adventures around Newtownabbey, Northern Ireland. Keep writing please! I want more Silly Billy!"*

*"Having met you as an adult, reading your adventures as a Silly Billy gave me an intimate view in to the child you were and the child that still twinkles in your eyes. The love of family that I always knew you had shines through in this beautiful series of stories that allowed me to travel back in time with you."*

- Christopher Nichol (age 13), and Michelle Chemerika, Winnipeg, Manitoba, Canada.

*"Do you know what I love about your books? They are written from a time when there was no computers and no electronic games. Childhood was simple then, although it wasn't simple for us. Every one of us remembers someone in our class trying to help others and getting into trouble at the same time.*

*In saying that, Greg uses his personal experience of being a child with subtle differences in Northern Ireland. Combining humour, 'Norn Ireland' dialect and creativity, Greg gives us an insight and reminder of being a child. Young or old, you will enjoy this unique insight into children in 1970's Norn Ireland."*

- Gráinne Clancy, Dublin, Ireland.

**Silly Billy and the Postage Stamp...**

*In this first adventure, and since his father is away at sea, Billy wants to be like his older brother who assumes the role of being the "Man of the House", and bosses his siblings around. Given a simple task of posting a letter to their father, this comical true-life story which is set in the community of Newtownabbey, Northern Ireland, captures the childhood experiences of Irish Author and Poet, Greg McVicker, in how one young boy can take a simple task and make a complete mess of it. The moral of this story is to not try covering up ones' countless mistakes and mishaps along the way as eventually they will be found out.*

**Silly Billy and the Good Deed...**

*In this second adventure, and since the tuck shop at his primary school is all sold out, Billy is asked to help his teacher get her favourite sweets along with his own reward. However, what should have taken only a few moments becomes an amusing escapade that is filled with numerous misfortunes due to Billy not following very specific directions. This hilarious true-life story which takes place in Newtownabbey, Northern Ireland, captures the childhood experiences of Irish Author and Poet, Greg McVicker, and his memories from years gone by. The moral of this story is to try your best, but to also do as one is told to do in the first place.*

**Silly Billy and the Escape from Carrick Castle...**

*In this third adventure, Billy is offered a chance to go fishing with his older brother and his mates alongside of the marina beside a Norman castle built in 1177 on the northern shores of Belfast Lough in Carrickfergus. Once there, however, fishing seems to be the last thing on their minds and leads to a troublesome chase within the confines of this mighty structure. This hysterical true-life reflection which took place in Newtownabbey, Northern Ireland, captures the childhood experiences of Irish Author and Poet, Greg McVicker. The moral of this story is that your freedom might not quite be your fate, especially when your father comes home.*

# The Adventures of
# Silly Billy

# The Adventures of Silly Billy

~~Trilogy~~: Volume 1

### GREG McVICKER, BSW.

Silly Billy and the Postage Stamp.

Silly Billy and the Good Deed.

Silly Billy and the Escape from Carrick Castle.

**The Adventures of Silly Billy**

by Greg McVicker, BSW.
Cover photo by gabo.
Cover Design by Trevor Harper.
Layout by Greg McVicker & Trevor Harper.

All rights reserved.

No part of this publication may be reproduced in any form, or by any means, electronic or mechanical, including photocopying, recording, or any information browsing, storing, or retrieval system, without permission in writing from the publisher.

ISBN:
978-1-7751622-4-7 (Softcover)
978-1-7751622-5-4 (eBook)

Produced by:

Belfast Child Publishing

# The Adventures of Silly Billy

The adventures of 'Silly Billy' started many years ago. Although he was named Gregory by his mummy and daddy when he was just a newborn baby, Gregory had a lot of mishaps while he was growing up. Some of those true-life stories are now on these pages, so they are.

By the way, and for whatever reason, people all across the North of Ireland will often end a sentence with 'so you are', 'so you have', 'so I did', or a combination of many other types of 'so...' As such, do not be surprised if you see several of those sayings at the end of sentences.

Before we get into the first of these three wee short stories about his childhood memories, Gregory would like you to know that 'Silly Billy' is a name that is often given to many children all throughout the North and South of Ireland, along with other parts of the United Kingdom including Scotland, Wales, and England when youngsters make mistakes. Gregory was infamous for making an awful lot of silly mistakes when he was a youngster, and would quite often be known as a 'Silly Billy'.

Thus, this book of short stories was written for all of the other Silly Billy's around the world. I am sure that there are lots of us who have had fun, memorable, yet quite silly missions, so there are!

Now, if you are sitting comfortably, then I'll begin...

# The Adventures of Silly Billy

## Silly Billy's Word Glossary:

Since I grew up in a wee country called Northern Ireland, I thought it would be best to let you know that we have our own version of the English language. You will see words in this story and might wonder what they mean (as was the case with a young lady named Katelyn; she looked them all up, so she did).

I hope this wee glossary (that is a ginormous word) helps all yousuns out. Your friendly neighbourhood, Silly Billy!

| | |
|---|---|
| Ma | My mummy, she is also called my mum. |
| Da | My daddy, he is also called my dad. |
| Kerb | Called a curb in other parts of the world. |
| Kerby | A kid's game. We stood on either side of the road and threw a |

# The Adventures of Silly Billy

|  |  |
|---|---|
|  | football at the other kerb to try and score points. It was dead brilliant. |
| Wee | Everything is wee in Norn Iron, so it is! |
| Norn Iron | Our wee way of saying Northern Ireland. |
| Tyre | A round thing made of squishy rubber. There are two on my brilliant bicycle and four on my ma's motor car, so there is. |
| Greengrocer | A person who has a wee shop that sells plants, fruits, vegetables, roses, garden tools, gnomes, and yucky smelly Brussels sprouts. |

# The Adventures of Silly Billy

**Chemist** — A person who has a wee shop that sells bokey red cough syrup and other medicines. They also have lots of stuff to make owee's all better.

**Lucozade** — Our granny brought us this fizzy drink to help make us feel better when we were sick. We drank that and had lots of Granny's tea, too. We would also get the Beano.

# The Adventures of Silly Billy

**Beano** — A brilliant wee comic book that we would look forward to reading on Wednesday's. Another cracker wee comic, Dandy, came on Monday. We would read about Dennis the Menace, his dog, Gnasher, Bully Beef and Chips, and Billy Whizz!

**Green Cross Code** — We learned this at school and would stop, look, and listen before we safely crossed the road. Darth Vader was the Green Cross Code man, so he was but he did not have his light sabre or any of his dark Jedi mind powers.

# The Adventures of Silly Billy

SILLY BILLY and the Postage Stamp

By Greg McVicker

# Silly Billy and the Postage Stamp

## Dedication:

This first story, ***Silly Billy and the Postage Stamp***, is dedicated to the beloved memory of my beautiful mum. An incredible lady, she sacrificed all that she had to protect her four asthmatic children in our hometown of Belfast, Northern Ireland, during our time growing up during a period that saw countless numbers of families affected by 'The Troubles.'

Our childhoods, which proved to be some of the happiest, yet most difficult days of our lives, continue to be extremely cherished and created blessed memories because of her undying efforts. Some of those memories are now being captured within the pages of this brilliant wee adventure.

I love you and miss you, mum…

– **Catherine Philomena McVicker.**
  **May 3, 1940 – May 11, 2005.**

# The Adventures of Silly Billy

Silly Billy had an older sister, Karen, an older brother, Joseph, and a wee sister named Angela. Together, along with their mum, Catherine, that his sisters, his brother, and he would call 'ma', they lived in their beautiful bungalow on Knockview Park. His dad, Charles, who they also knew as their 'da', worked as a Chief Cook on ships at sea. Although he was not home very often, he would write a bunch of letters and would telephone them all when his ship was docked. Billy missed him, but knew that his dad was working very hard so that he, and his family, could eat good food, have a nice house to live in, clean clothes to wear, and fun toys to play with which Billy's dad would bring home from sea.

One of the most favourite things that Billy and his sisters and brother would look forwards too was what his dad would be bringing home next. It was always a great surprise, one that kept them all in suspense until their father decided that it was time to show them all what he had found on his travels.

# Silly Billy and the Postage Stamp

Billy's mum, Catherine, would often ask him, Karen, Joseph, and Angela, to help with chores around the house including cleaning their bedrooms, washing, drying, and stowing the dishes, or running errands for their granny. It was usually Billy who did the errands for his granny, which he did just as the Heavens opened up as his mum would often say with its latest torrential downpour of rain. For this, Billy and his siblings would all receive pocket money at the end of each week to buy sweets.

Since Karen was the oldest, she would help her mum cook dinner. Joseph, being the oldest boy, boasted that while their father, Charles, worked on ships at sea, he was the 'man of the house'. Because of this, Joseph loved to give out orders and boss everyone around. He would help his mum to cut the grass, or would use his dad's tools to fix things. Since she was much younger, Billy's sister, Angela, played with her dolls instead of helping Karen to keep their room clean for which Karen would get upset with her, so she did.

# The Adventures of Silly Billy

One day, while he was out playing on the slide and swing set in the back garden of their home, Billy's mum asked him to help her. She wanted him to go to the Woodford Shops, which were close to where they lived and gave him a special set of instructions.

"Now Billy," said his mum. "Here is what I would like for you to do. I need you to buy a bottle of hairspray, one stamp, and to post this letter to your dad for me."

Billy was very excited. Although he would often go to the shops with his mum, she would be the one to buy stamps and other items, along with posting letters to his father. Billy felt that this was his chance to be a grown up and to show his older and very bossy brother, Joseph, that he too could be the man of the house. Billy had actually hoped that Joseph wouldn't be able to boss him around anymore, and so he leapt at this opportunity, so he did.

Billy repeated what his mum wanted him to do, put on his guddies, took his coat from the wardrobe, and went into the garage to

## Silly Billy and the Postage Stamp

get his bicycle. Oh, Billy's bicycle... it was a beautiful bike that he had named 'Thunder'. He jumped on the seat, kicked back the stand, and went to start peddling. He didn't get very far though as Billy had forgotten that Thunder's tyre had become punctured the day before.

"I'm sorry, Thunder," said Billy. "I am not able to take you with me today to do this special job for my ma. Perhaps next time, after I get you fixed. You know what this means. I will need to ask for some help."

Billy sighed. Joseph was the only one who knew how to fix bikes. He would often take spoons from the kitchen drawer, and would use them to remove the tyre from the wheel before repairing the inner tube when it got a puncture. He knew everything that needed to be done. Joseph was always faster and better at fixing things, so he was.

After placing Thunder back up against the wall, Billy thought about using Karen's bike. He remembered though that the last time he took it without first asking her

## The Adventures of Silly Billy

permission, he got in a lot of trouble for doing so. Once more, Billy sighed.

"I guess I will have to walk to the shops," he said, before making his way up the driveway and onto the footpath outside his house. He did not like walking, as it always took much longer than if he were to take Thunder, so it did.

Billy was passing his neighbours home, which used to belong to his Aunt Maureen and Uncle Malcolm before they moved to Nova Scotia, Canada, when he heard his name being called.

"Billy," said his mum. "You left the letter and the money on the kitchen table."

"Whoops," thought Billy. He was so excited to do his grown-up work that he had forgotten to get the items he needed to complete this big job. Billy turned around and made his way to the house. But, rather than walk back down the footpath outside of their house to the top of his driveway, he climbed over the wall and onto

## Silly Billy and the Postage Stamp

the rockery, all the while trying to avoid stepping on his mum's flowers. Catherine took great pride in making her garden look beautiful, and spent several hours working on it. Her favourite rose colour was peach. She also had white, yellow, red, and pink roses too.

"Careful," said Billy's mum. "I don't want you falling."

"I'll be fine, ma, so I will," said Billy. However, his foot slipped off of the rock and into the freshly turned soil that his mum had just done that morning, leaving behind a **BIG** footprint. However, and instead of falling forward and onto the soft grass, Billy ended up stepping on more soil and bumped into some of his mum's roses causing **SEVERAL** petals to fall off. Billy tried to pick the petals up, only to get his arms scratched by the thorns from the rose bushes.

Letting out a yelp before losing his balance and, as if in slow motion, his mum watched as her carefully pruned roses

# The Adventures of Silly Billy

became **SCATTERED** all over the flowerbed. By the time Billy was done, it looked like a tornado had touched down onto this one area of their home.

Jumping down to the garden path, Billy tried removing his footprints from the soil with his hands, leaving them **COVERED** in mud. He walked towards his mum, whistling while pretending that nothing had happened.

His mum, who was standing at the front door, said, "I wish you would not be such a Silly Billy, and use the driveway instead of the rockery. How many times do you need to be told? Look at my poor roses. It will take me ages to clean them up. And would you look at the dirt of your hands. **FOR GOODNESS SAKE, DON'T WIPE THEM ON YOUR CLOTHES. I'M ONLY JUST FINISHED WASHING THEM**... Oh, what's the point? I may as well be talking to the wall."

Catherine would often say this while speaking to him. Although he tried to do the same thing many times, Billy could not understand why the wall never spoke back.

# Silly Billy and the Postage Stamp

Since his mum had told Karen, Joseph, Angela, and Billy that she had eyes on the back of her head and knew everything they were doing, good or bad, Billy believed that his mum had magical powers. It seemed that his friend's mums also did the same, and that they too had the same magical powers as his mum.

When he reached the front door and as she tried to clean up the muddy handprints from his trousers, Billy looked over his shoulder and could see the mess that he had made of his mum's flowers.

"Sorry, ma," said Billy. "Once I am done my big job, I will get the vacuum cleaner out and vacuum up all the petals, so I will..."

Hearing this, Billy's mum took a deep breath and let out a **HUGE** sigh while saying, "Goodness, gracious me. I don't know what to say. When will you ever learn?"

Billy made his way back up the steps and towards the rockery. He remembered what his mum had just told him. To try and

## The Adventures of Silly Billy

make her forget about what just happened, and, in hoping that she would see he could follow her instructions, Billy changed direction and walked along the garden path. Although, and as he was so lost in thought about what his mum might tell the wall about all of the silly mistakes that he had just made, he tripped over his own two feet and fell into the driveway.

"I'm alright, ma, so I am," shouted Billy, even though he now had a few scrapes on his hands.

His mum shook her head and said, "Tut, Tut, Tut, Tut, Tut." She then placed her hands on her sides, looked up towards the Heavens as she often did and in a low voice, said, "Good Lord above. Please give me the strength to get through this day. Boys will be boys, but my son is definitely a Silly Billy. Do you think that he will ever learn?"

Hearing this, Billy wondered if the clouds or perhaps the good Lord above would speak to her since his ma could already talk to walls.

## Silly Billy and the Postage Stamp

Billy got off of the ground and made his way towards the footpath that ran along the front of their house. He skipped from one foot onto the other all the while making up and singing a song that he was taught for a school play called 'The Belle of Belfast City.' Being the cheeky wee article that he was, Billy would always change the words...

> "I'll tell me ma, when I get home. I've done my chores, so leave me alone. I walked real far, without my bike, and that was such a dreadful hike. I am handsome, I am Silly; I am Billy from Belfast City. I'll get married when I'm eighty-three, yer ma's yer da! Ack, what about ye?"

Billy felt very proud about how he could make up his own lyrics to this very popular song, which would make his adventure to the shops much more fun. Even though the shops were not far from where he lived, he thought of himself as being a grown up as he passed each house along his street.

# The Adventures of Silly Billy

While walking, he looked back to see his own house fall further into the distance away from him. Billy also saw that his mum was watching him and began waving to her.

Billy's mum waved her arms all around in the air, pointed, and began shouting up to him. As he was humming and singing his own wee song, he could not hear what she was saying. Just as Billy turned around...

**BOOM. "YEOWCH!"**

Since he was not paying attention as to where he was going, Billy walked straight into a lamppost, bumping his forehead, and leaving a **HUGE LUMP** in its place.

"Who would be silly enough to put a lamppost on a footpath," said Billy, as his head throbbed, and his nose stung. Billy could feel tears welling up in his eyes. He then made a poor choice and decided to kick the lamppost thinking that it would make things better, only to now have his foot hurting just as badly.

**"OUCH!"**

## Silly Billy and the Postage Stamp

Seeing stars flash in front of his eyes for a moment, Billy hopped around on one leg, holding his sore foot in one hand while his other hand covered the swelling lump that was growing bigger by the second on his forehead. He wanted his mum to be proud of him, although he realized that she would have probably been calling him a "right buck eejit" about now. This did not make Billy's head or foot feel any better, so it didn't.

Billy realized that he needed to hurry up and get moving along if he were to complete his big job. Limping a little and while he whimpered from the pain, Billy continued on his way. Due to his latest mishaps, he had forgotten that he had already managed to climb the steep hill of Knockview Park. This was one of two huge hills that he would have to conquer. The next street over from his, called Knockview Avenue, also had a steep hill to it which would often leave Billy stopping to catch his breath, so it did.

# The Adventures of Silly Billy

When he reached the top of his street, Billy stopped to think for a moment about the safest route that he could take. He counted on his fingers and at the same time, pointed in several different directions. This made it look like he was the conductor for an orchestra. Billy then spoke out loud as if he were talking to someone.

"Hmmm. If I go that way, I will have to cross one, two, three, four different streets to get to the shops." Billy then thought about the other route he knew and started pointing and counting all over again.

"If I go this way, I will have to cross Knockview Road, Knockview Gardens, and the Woodford Road before I reach the shops. That's only three streets and would be much quicker for me, so it would."

After choosing the shorter of the two routes, Billy remembered what he was taught in primary school – to use the Green Cross Code. This was to ensure that parents, and their kids, were always safe when crossing the street.

## Silly Billy and the Postage Stamp

Billy stopped with his two feet behind the kerb. He looked to the right, then to the left, and back to the right again. Seeing that the road was clear, he made his way across the Knockview Road while constantly looking back and forth to make sure that there were no vehicles coming his way.

Upon reaching the footpath on the other side, Billy noticed that Mr. Graham, an elderly man who had lived in the neighbourhood for as long as he could remember, was outside working on his garden. He took tremendous pride with his prize-winning flowers, so he did.

"Hello, Mr. Graham," said Billy.

"Hello, Silly Billy," said Mr. Graham. "Where are you off to today?"

"I'm going up to the shops for my ma, so I am," replied Billy. "She gave me a grown-up job to do, so she did. I'll be there in no time at all." Billy showed Mr. Graham the letter that was addressed to his dad.

# The Adventures of Silly Billy

"Good for you," replied Mr. Graham. "You must be the man of the house now."

Billy's face turned a bright shade of red at what Mr. Graham had just said, and felt as if he had suddenly grown two feet taller! Billy explained what had happened to him back at his house with his mum's rose bushes, getting mud on his hands, Thunder having a flat tyre, not wanting to take his sisters' bike, and how the lamppost attacked him for no reason. Billy pointed to the lump on his head while he told Mr. Graham about how he kicked the lamppost to teach it a lesson, only for it to cause him pain a second time.

Seeing this, Mr. Graham offered to get Billy a tissue with an ice cube in it, just as his mum would do. As he waited outside, Mr. Graham informed Billy he would be right back and disappeared into his house.

Billy noticed that Mrs. Graham was sitting in her favourite rocking chair in the living room. Just as he always did, Billy

## Silly Billy and the Postage Stamp

gave her a wave and then a big smile. Mrs. Graham waved and smiled back.

Mr. Graham came back out with the ice cube in the tissue, gave it to Billy, told him to be a little more careful, wished him well, and went back to working in his prized garden.

After thanking him for his help, Billy thought that it would be a good idea and decided to tuck the letter into his pocket since he now needed to hold onto the ice and tissue.

Slowly walking along Knockview Avenue and with the lump on his head starting to become freezing cold from the ice, Billy realized perhaps he had spoken with Mr. Graham a little too long and that he would need to hurry up to get his big job done.

"I should already be at the bend before the big hill, so I should" said Billy out loud, and decided to run past the next three houses all the while holding the tissue and ice to his bump.

## The Adventures of Silly Billy

"Number six... number eight... number ten... There we go," said Billy. "That should do it. Now I can walk and skip again, so I can."

A few more houses went past. By this time, Billy had reached the second hill at the middle of Knockview Avenue. He knew that his legs would get tired from walking up this part of the road, so he decided that he would pace himself.

"I can do this. If I walk harder and faster, I will get there a lot sooner, so I will."

Billy started walking as quickly as he could. In no time at all, his legs became tired and sore. He found himself walking a lot slower than what he had originally started. While passing house number sixteen, he began huffing and puffing. Billy stopped for a moment to catch his breath but was determined to reach the shops.

When he reached the top of the Knockview Avenue, Billy would now have to cross Knockview Gardens as well. He could

## Silly Billy and the Postage Stamp

clearly see the Woodford Shops ahead of him. For whatever reason, he said the name of each one as loud as he could, almost as if he were shouting at them for not being closer to his home.

"The Hair Dressers, the Greengrocers, the Chemists, the Post Office, and then that is the Spar, so it is."

A couple of people who were about to walk into their house heard Billy and said, "Are you alright, wee lad?"

Billy looked around to see whom they were speaking to. He did not realize that it was him who was making such a racket. He then heard the people mutter, "Ack, he's probably not wise in the head, so he's not." Billy would hear his granny say this from time to time when she was talking with his mum and would often wonder what they meant by this, although his mum would tell him from time to time, "Ack, your head's cut, so it is."

## The Adventures of Silly Billy

Once again, Billy took a moment to remember what his school had taught him about crossing the street on his own. But, before doing so, he decided to take a little more time as the muscles in his legs felt like they had turned to jelly from walking this far.

Upon reaching the other side, Billy counted the remaining homes he would need to pass. There were only **four** houses left. He was **very happy** that he had made it this far and would soon prove to his mum he could do his **own** grown up chores. He skipped along, as it seemed to be faster and easier than walking. Carefully checking for cars again, Billy crossed the last of the streets, the Woodford Road.

Reaching the Woodford Shops, Billy jumped. In front of him was the tall, red letterbox that stood just outside of the Greengrocers. Jim, the owner, was putting out wooden crates that were stuffed with lots of fresh vegetables. Billy then watched

## Silly Billy and the Postage Stamp

as he put down a big box of Brussels sprouts and in his loudest voice, said **"YUCK!"**

Hearing this, Jim waved and walked over to greet Billy.

"Hello, Mr. Silly Billy. What brings you to the shops? What happened to your head? Did you have a fall? You have a bit of a bump, so you do. And how come you don't like Brussels sprouts?"

Billy told Jim about the very important chores that his mum wanted him to do. He then told Jim about falling off the rockery, Thunder having a flat tyre, knocking the petals off his mum's roses, bumping his head into the lamppost and then kicking it for hurting him, which hurt even more, and that Mr. Graham had given him an ice cube in a tissue.

Staring at the pile of fresh vegetables, he then went on to tell Jim why Brussels sprouts were **YUCKY!** Billy described them as being "tiny, green, bokey, smelly cabbages" and that he would hold his nose

# The Adventures of Silly Billy

when they were made for dinner. The reason for his dislike of them is that the last time his dad was home from sea, he made him eat three of them even though his mum knew that he did not like them. Billy became sick and completely ruined his Sunday dinner.

Jim looked at Billy's head and said, "Mr. Graham did the right thing for you, young man. You need to be more careful and not make so many mistakes. Can you let your mum know that if she needs new roses, I can order them in for her, so I can."

"Aye, no bother," said Billy, and turned to walk away. Jim stopped him. "And by the way, before you go. Be sure you eat your vegetables. They'll make you big and strong and put hair on your chest."

Billy face went red as he was always told that he was a fussy eater. He looked down and back up again before saying, "But I don't want hair on my chest. That's why I only eat peas and carrots."

## Silly Billy and the Postage Stamp

Jim gave a hearty laugh as Billy's face turned a deeper shade of red. Billy paused for a second, and then continued to share his thoughts.

"Ack, sure, I'll tell me ma, when I get home, that you've got roses, and a garden gnome."

Jim gave him a funny look and said, "Mind your manners, son. Knock that off, now, will ye."

Billy stopped singing on the spot. He realized that Jim probably did not like the fact that he was making up a cheeky wee song about his shop and apologised.

He turned to look at the red letterbox, winked and smiled, and then gave it two thumbs up. It had a big job to do collecting everyone's post. Soon, the letter that his mum had given him would go inside of it and would be on its way to his father.

"I bet my da will be excited to get my ma's letter, so he will," said Billy, and tried

## The Adventures of Silly Billy

to repeat the important list that his mum had given to him to do.

"Stamp the hairspray, post the ice cube, and buy a letter."

Billy thought hard for a second and said, "Wait a minute. That doesn't sound right? I'm sure my ma told me something different, so she did. What did she want me to do?"

Since he had spent so much time telling Mr. Graham and Jim the Greengrocer all about the mistakes he made, Billy realized that he had forgotten everything that his mum had wanted him to do.

Billy decided to walk towards the Chemists. The owner, named Joe, was filling prescriptions at the back of the shop. His assistant, Dorothy, who was also Joe's wife, was placing supplies on the shelves. Upon seeing him entering the shop, Dorothy turned to speak to him.

"Hi Silly Billy, are you here to pick up some cough syrup? Your mum was telling me

# Silly Billy and the Postage Stamp

a few days ago that your younger sister, Angela, has whooping cough. She said she was taking her to see Dr. Farrell down at the Whiteabbey Hospital."

"Aye, she does indeed," said Billy. "But I think my ma already picked up her medicine. She gave her a spoonful from a brown bottle in the refrigerator this morning. I think it might be the same medicine that we get sometimes, it's a red liquid that tastes like boke, so it does."

"Oh?" replied Dorothy. "I suppose that Joe must have gotten that sorted for her already. He hasn't said anything just yet as he has been busy and hasn't had a moment to have his tea. Well then. What is it that I can do to help you out today?"

Billy told Dorothy how his mum had given him a very important grown up job to do, but he could not remember what that was. He felt bad, as he did not want to disappoint his mum. Dorothy asked Billy to take a deep breath and to see if he could tell her what his chore was.

# The Adventures of Silly Billy

"My ma asked if I could stamp an ice cube, post some hairspray, and buy a letter," said Billy.

Dorothy gave Billy a puzzled look and said, "What? Are you sure that is what your mum wanted you to do? That doesn't sound right to me, so it doesn't. Do you want me to ring and ask what she needs? I wonder if that bump on your head has made you forget?"

"Ack, no," replied Billy with a panicked voice. He explained that if Dorothy rang his mum, she would not ask him to do any more grown up chores. Dorothy knew that Billy always wanted to be the man of the house, just like his older brother.

"Right then, Billy" said Dorothy. "Let's see if we can figure this out together. Can you tell me again what your mum has asked for?"

She took out a blank piece of paper and wrote down what Billy told her a second time, which was still wrong. After looking at the words, Dorothy said, "I think I've got it. Your mum needs you to buy some

## Silly Billy and the Postage Stamp

hairspray and a stamp. I am not sure about the ice cube though. Did you bring a letter with you to post?"

"Aye, she did," said Billy.

He put his hand in his pocket, only to pull out a very crumpled and now sopping wet envelope.

"Oh oh," said Dorothy. "What in God's green earth happened to this poor letter? It looks like it has been put through with the washing, so it does."

While she tried her best to straighten it out for him, Billy expected her to look up to the ceiling just like his mum would do and waited to see if she would get a response from the good Lord above. Thankfully, nothing happened.

Billy explained all the events that had unfolded while he was making his way to the shops, and that Mr. Graham had given him some ice to help with the lump on his head. Billy then told Dorothy that as his hand was getting cold and red from holding the

## The Adventures of Silly Billy

ice cube too long and that the tissue was getting very wet, he would switch hands. Billy went on to say that as he was told to never litter, he put the tissue in his pocket – the **SAME** pocket that he had put the letter in so that it would not get lost. He thought that this was a great idea. It would have been without the ice cube being in the same pocket.

With a disappointed look on his face, Billy looked at the ground and shuffled his feet. He could not remember the brand of hairspray his mum wanted him to buy, nor did he want to disappoint her. Dorothy asked if Billy would know what kind it was from looking at the different bottles on the shelf.

"Aye," said Billy, as he brightened up and immediately stopped shuffling. "That would be brilliant, so it would."

After scanning the shelves, he pointed out which bottle his mum had wanted. Just as Dorothy put it into a paper bag for him, he placed the money on the counter.

# Silly Billy and the Postage Stamp

"Thanks for your help," said Billy.

"You are most welcome," she replied. "Do you need anything else?"

Billy thought carefully for a moment and said, "Well, I need to get that stamp now but I have to go next door to the post office for that, so I do. Thank you for all of your help. But, would you mind not telling my ma that I forgot what I was supposed to do for her?"

Dorothy smiled and said, "Well Billy, it's not right to keep secrets from your mum, so it's not. But, this one time only, I won't tell her that you forgot. Now, on you go. Mind yourself and be careful. No more silly mistakes, now, you hear?"

He thanked Dorothy once more and made his way from the Chemists over to the Post Office. There, the shopkeeper, Eileen, greeted him.

"Hi Silly Billy," said Eileen. "What can I do to give you a wee hand today? Or are you in to get a few sweets from your pocket money?"

# The Adventures of Silly Billy

He told Eileen how his mum had given him an important grown up job to do and that he would need to buy a stamp and post a letter to his father. "I already bought the hairspray from the Chemists, so I did," said Billy. "And I didn't forget to do anything." Billy knew that he was telling a fib.

"Good for you for doing such a good job, well done," said Eileen. "Now, would you like a first class or a second class stamp?"

"I don't know," replied Billy. "My ma said I needed a stamp. Does it really matter what kind of a stamp it needs?"

Seeing that Billy was carrying a letter, Eileen asked if she could look at the address on the front of the envelope.

"Oh, this is going to your dad overseas," said Eileen. You will definitely need a first class stamp for that otherwise it will never reach him. That will be 99p. Boy, I have never seen such a wrinkled letter as this one. What happened to it?"

## Silly Billy and the Postage Stamp

"Thank you," said Billy, putting the money on the counter and did not answer the question Eileen had just asked. He smiled since he knew that the last grown up chore he needed to do was to post the letter.

Billy left the shop and walked over to the big, red letterbox. He looked to see what time the postman would come to pick up the post.

"Ah, he'll be here around half five o'clock, so he will," said Billy. Standing on his tiptoes since he was not tall enough, he pushed the envelope into the opening of the letterbox and kept pushing it until he could no longer feel it on his fingertips.

"There we go," said Billy. "Pretty soon, my da will receive that wee letter from my ma. Maybe the next time she writes, she can tell him all about how I have become the man of the house. Joseph won't be able to boss me around any longer, so he won't. I'll be the man of the house, so I will."

# The Adventures of Silly Billy

Billy was excited to get home. He checked the Woodford Road to make sure it was safe to cross. He thought this part of his journey home would be so much easier and faster, as he would not have to climb any hills but simply go down them. Sure enough, and in no time at all, Billy found himself waving to Mrs. Graham once again. Mr. Graham must have finished all the work in his garden, as he was nowhere to be seen.

After crossing Knockview Road, Billy stood at the top of his street, Knockview Park. He stopped for a moment and looked out across to Belfast Lough. It looked so peaceful. Billy loved the beauty of this, and could see the town of Bangor in the distance. A tanker ship was floating towards its dock. Billy knew his dad sailed on different ships from the ones he often saw coming and going from Belfast.

Taking a deep breath, he sighed and started walking home again as he knew that his dad would sail into Larne on the Sealink Ferries. Along with his mum, Karen, Joseph,

## Silly Billy and the Postage Stamp

and Angela, Billy would always go to pick his father up and would wait with excitement to see him coming down the gangplank.

Billy made his way on down the hill. He stopped for a moment to wave to his Aunt May and Uncle Roy who lived at number nine. Billy knew all of the neighbours who lived on the street, and took pride that he could stop and say hello to each of them. Although they were not really his aunt or his uncle, Billy, his sisters, and his brother had always called them as such as they would often come down to the house to visit with his mum while their dad was away at sea. Sometimes, when Joseph was not available to help Billy fix Thunder after getting a flat tyre, his Uncle Roy would offer to do so.

Reaching the rockery, Billy carefully stepped onto the rocks and once again made a **HUGE** footprint in the soil while knocking more rose petals off.

"Whoops," said Billy. He looked around to see if his mum had seen him make this

# The Adventures of Silly Billy

mistake again. No, she was not there this time. Billy thought that he should not clean up his footprint otherwise his mum would know that he had done something wrong again since he would have mud on his hands and most likely, all over his clothes.

"Phew," thought Billy as he climbed over yet another wall and followed the pathway to the back of his house. What Billy did not notice though was that his mum had already cleaned up his mess from earlier. Many of her roses looked so much smaller now, as several of their petals were missing.

Billy walked in to the kitchen and found that his mum and Karen were cooking dinner. A pot of potatoes was boiling on the cooker, with peas and carrots for him, and Brussels sprouts for everyone else. Billy would have held his nose shut if it were not for the wonderful aroma of a Steak and Kidney pie drifting from the oven. Except for the tiny, green, bokey, smelly cabbages, everything else smelled wonderful and made Billy's tummy growl.

# Silly Billy and the Postage Stamp

"I could eat a horse right now, so I could," said Billy.

"You're back? Good," said his mum. "Did you get me some hairspray and post the letter?"

With a huge smile, Billy gave his mum a paper bag that had a bottle of hairspray inside. After he put the change on the table, he proudly sang a wee song.

"I'll tell me ma, when I get home, I posted the letter, it's not going to Rome..."

Billy's mum interrupted his singing. "Would you quit actin' the eejit. Did you get what I asked you for?"

"Ack aye, I did rightly, so I did," said Billy. "I posted the letter to da. Oh, aye, ma, before I forget, here's your stamp too."

Billy's mum looked at him; her eyes wide open in disbelief. Karen looked at her mum with her eyes wide open as well. Karen also opened her mouth to speak but no sounds came out. They both looked at each other, and then back at Billy. Finally, it was his mum who would break the silence between the three of them. In an exasperated voice, she said, "You did what? You posted... the letter... without the stamp?"

Billy looked at his mum and said, "Sure, aye. You told me to buy hairspray, to buy a stamp, and to post the letter. You never said to put the stamp on it. I didn't know, so I didn't."

Karen shook her head and said, "Ack sure, Ma, you may as well have been talking to the wall."

"Good Lord above. You are such a Silly Billy," said his mum. "Without a stamp, the letter will never reach your dad. What are we going to do? Goodness gracious, can I not get you to do a simple chore for me. Let me think here for a wee minute."

Billy hesitated for a moment and waited to see if the good Lord above was going to say, "Tut, Tut, Tut." His cheeks turned a bright shade of red for a third time while his mum looked at the clock.

## Silly Billy and the Postage Stamp

"What time does the postman come at?" she wondered aloud.

Billy remembered that he had checked the times on the big, red letterbox. "The postman comes at half five o'clock, so he does," said Billy. "I read that, so I did."

His mum corrected him. "You mean half five. Good, we still have time. Billy, while Karen and I continue making the dinner, you will need to walk back to the shops. Wait for the postman and then tell him that you posted the letter without the stamp you just bought. You will need to find the letter, put the stamp **ONTO** it, and then post it again."

Although this seemed like a bigger set of instructions than Billy was first given to do, he knew that he had to make things right if his mum were to tell his dad all about his grown-up chores if he were to become the man of the house and not have his older brother boss him around.

"Alright ma," said Billy, and off he set once again.

# The Adventures of Silly Billy

Making sure that his mum was not watching him, Billy climbed back over the rockery only this time he was sure to not hit any rose petals or leave more footprints in the soil. He started into a slight run but again found the hill on his street made his legs feel like they always did, as if they were made of jelly. Billy used all his strength and began running until he reached the top of Knockview Park.

This time, after crossing Knockview Road over to Knockview Avenue, he did not see Mr. or Mrs. Graham. Walking along the footpath, Billy wondered what might happen if the postman were to come early, and if he did, would leave the letter without the stamp on it behind? As Billy did not want this to happen, he started running only to realize that he had to get up the second huge hill once more.

His muscles started to burn as if he had walked on hot coals and his legs had been set on fire.

# Silly Billy and the Postage Stamp

Panting and out of breath, Billy reached Knockview Gardens and there, in the near distance, was the Woodford Shops. Billy checked the road and using his Green Cross Code skills, made his way across, past the final four houses to the Woodford Road, and over to the big, red letterbox once again.

Billy stared at it, smiled, winked, gave two thumbs up and expected the door on the front of it to open and for the envelope to jump out. No such luck. The door was locked. He then tried sticking his finger into the keyhole but that didn't help either as it got pinched. He stood on his tiptoes to see if he could find the letter at the slot where he had placed it, but again, no such luck.

Billy then thought if he could perhaps use the same magical powers that his mum and many of his friend's mums had, in that they were all able to talk to walls and to the good Lord above, that he could easily solve this problem. He took a deep breath, closed his eyes, and thought about what he should say.

# The Adventures of Silly Billy

"Right, here goes. Hey there. Would you open your door so I can put a stamp on my da's letter?"

After waiting for a moment and then opening his eyes, he saw that nothing had happened. Billy thought about what he had just said and realized that he never used any of the magic words he was taught. Once again, he closed his eyes, took a deep breath, and spoke.

"Dear Mr. Letterbox. My name is Greg, but everyone calls me Silly Billy. Could you please open your door so I can put a stamp on a letter to my da. Pretty please! My ma never told me that I needed to do this. Then I can go home. Pretty, pretty please?! I'm so hungry and could eat a horse, so I could. Thank you."

Billy believed that using the magic word 'please' at least three times would help solve his problem. Still, nothing happened.

He took a seat on the wall, took the stamp out of his pocket, and stared at it.

## Silly Billy and the Postage Stamp

He thought about what magic words he might try to perhaps have the stamp find its way to his dad's letter. Abracadabra? Hocus Pocus? Hey, Presto? Open Sesame? As he did, other people came up and put their envelopes into the letterbox. However, all of theirs had stamps on them.

Just as Billy began daydreaming about what else might work, suddenly, a man in a black coat and a black hat with lots of keys walked over to the letterbox. He did not seem to notice that Billy was sitting nearby waiting for him as he was singing away to himself...

> "I'll tell me ma, when I go home, the boys won't leave the girls alone. They pulled my hair, they stole my comb, but that's all right, 'til I go home. She is handsome, she is pretty, she is the Belle of Belfast City. She is courting, one two three, please won't you tell me who is she?"

# The Adventures of Silly Billy

Billy jumped. He was about to say that his version of this famous song was so much better until he realized that the person in the black coat was Alfie the Postman!

Billy watched as Alfie found the perfect key to open the front door of the letterbox. Finally, he would be able to get the letter back, fix his mistake, and make everything perfect.

Billy skipped up to him and told him all about how his mum had asked him to do a grown-up job. How he had bought the hairspray, bought the stamp, and posted the letter to his dad... but did not put the stamp on it. Billy went as far to describe the envelope – there were red and blue stripes around the outside edge and it also had the word 'Air Mail' written on the front of it.

As he did so, Billy was shocked to see that his envelope was not the first one to come out of the letterbox. He tried to count, but there were hundreds of letters, all different shapes, sizes, and colours.

## Silly Billy and the Postage Stamp

As soon as Alfie started placing the letters into his beige sack, Billy spotted his envelope and shouted at the top of his lungs...

**"THERE IT IS! I SEE IT, SO I DO. IT'S THE ONE WITHOUT THE POSTAGE STAMP ON IT!"**

Alfie asked Billy to not shout as people would ask him if he was alright in the head before asking him if he was sure this was the right one. Billy looked at the writing on the outside of the envelope and said, "Yes, that is the right one. That is my mum's writing. I know because she always writes like that and she used a blue pen." Alfie chuckled, as his dad's name, Charles, was clearly written on the front.

Billy took the stamp from his pocket, licked the back of it and as it tasted so awful, said **YUCK** as loud as he could! He stuck the stamp onto the front, right corner of the envelope, took his sleeve, and then wiped his tongue on it to try and get rid of the horrible taste.

# The Adventures of Silly Billy

"Here you go," said Billy proudly. "My job is now done, so it is!"

Alfie took the envelope, looked at it, gasped, and said, "You Silly Billy. You put the stamp on **UPSIDE DOWN**, so you did!"

Billy looked down at the ground, took a deep breath, and shuffled his feet before letting out a soft groan.

"Oh no. If I tell my mum that I put the stamp on upside down, she will think I cannot do a grown-up job properly. With me making so many mistakes today, she will **NEVER** ask me to be the man of the house. Now my brother will boss me all over the place again, so he will."

Seeing that Billy was quite upset, Alfie reassured him.

"It's alright. My friends and I at the post office will make sure that this letter gets to your dad. Don't worry. Everything will be just fine. I promise you that, so I do."

## Silly Billy and the Postage Stamp

Once again, Billy's cheeks turned a rosy shade, but he was sure to use his manners.

"Thank you very much," said Billy.

He watched as Alfie placed the last of the envelopes into the beige sack, closed the door so that it could get more letters, and locked it with his set of keys.

"Well, it is now just after half five and that is my last stop of the day, so it is," said Alfie, as he put the sack into the back of his van.

Billy stood and waved as he watched the red van drive down the Woodford Road with the letter addressed to his dad. He walked towards the kerb and ensuring that he followed all his Green Cross Code instructions, happily skipped his way home so he could enjoy a Steak and Kidney dinner with potatoes, peas, and carrots. He thought it would be best if he held his nose so that he did not have to smell the stinky, yucky, and very bokey Brussels sprouts.

*****

# The Adventures of Silly Billy

A few months after he had completed his big job, Billy picked up the post that had dropped through the letterbox of his home and gave it to his mum. She saw that there was a letter from Charles. Billy patiently waited, as his dad would always start his letters by asking how his mum, his two sisters, his brother, and how he himself were doing. Carefully, she opened the letter and started to read aloud.

"Dear Catherine. Thank you for your wonderful letter…" it began. "Since things are going very well out here at sea, I'll ask you how the kids and yourself are doing in just a wee moment. However, I thought you should know that for some reason, the first thing I saw when your letter arrived on my ship is that it was severely crumpled as if someone had stuffed it into their pocket. That has never happened before. But do you know what I found to be really strange. I don't know if someone was playing a joke on me, but the stamp on the front of the envelope was upside down…"

# Silly Billy and the Postage Stamp

Well, that is my story about the Postage Stamp. To all of the kids out there and who are reading this wee book with your family, don't be a Silly Billy. Always try your hardest and listen to your parents or caregivers so that you can be the best you can be. My mum always believed in my efforts even though I made countless mistakes with everything I tried to do. But, I guess that is what made things such a wonderful adventure, so I do!

I never did become the man of the house. My sisters and I would call our brother bossy boots as he bossed us around when our dad was away at sea. Even when our dad was home and we would be out playing, he would still boss us around, so he would!

## THE END

# The Adventures of Silly Billy

SILLY BILLY and the Good Deed

By Greg McVicker

# Silly Billy and the Good Deed

## Dedication:

This second story, ***Silly Billy and the Good Deed***, is dedicated to the memory of my beloved sister. Diagnosed with Acute Lymphoblastic Leukaemia in September 2011, she began to wage a courageous battle that only a determined Celtic Woman could do in wanting to defeat this life-threatening disease. Successful in her initial efforts, and without ever questioning why she was chosen to take on this monumental challenge, she relapsed. In the face of adversity, this warrior fought through to her final moments until she was finally called to join our mum.

Although she spent forty-eight years on this earth, a timeframe that was far too young and much too short by all measurements, those who were lucky enough to be enriched by her worldview, love, and knowledge, can certainly count each and every one of those blessings. Fortunately for me, I was blessed to be her brother…

Rest In Peace, sis. I love you, I miss you, and as I have before, only the Creator knows how much my heart breaks each day.

**– Karen Theresa McVicker.**
**May 17, 1967 – November 8, 2015.**

# The Adventures of Silly Billy

One of Billy's most prized possessions that his mum and dad had bought him and his brother, Joseph, were a pair of matching bicycles. Billy decided to name his "Thunder". A Raleigh Chopper, Thunder was a beautiful shade of deep purple, while Joseph's was bright red. They had a large wheel at the back, a small wheel at the front, chopper style handlebars, and a long seat that could be used to carry a schoolbag or a friend.

As a gearbox with a big red handle sat in the middle of the frame, the bike had three different speeds: first (easiest), second (medium), and third (hardest). As his neighbourhood had so many hills, Billy preferred to keep Thunder in first or second gear, and would only shift into third gear when he could pedal fast. Usually, this was when he was going down a steep hill, as it was so much easier than going up them.

When Billy did manage to get Thunder into third gear and since the wind flowed past him with such incredible force, he

## Silly Billy and the Good Deed

felt like he had superpowers and could fly. Often, Billy had dreams where he could do just that, spreading his arms out like an aeroplane and by moving them ever so slightly, he could soar high into the air as if he was an eagle or fly low to the ground.

One day, Billy decided that he would take his bike to his primary school. After he had gone into the garage to get Thunder, Billy's mum, Catherine, reminded him of a few very important rules that he needed to follow each and every time:

1. The first was to ride carefully.

2. The second was to use the Green Cross Code when he was crossing each street to get to his school.

3. Lastly, for Billy to please watch out for pedestrians and other vehicles. Knowing that he made mistakes that would lead to several mishaps, Catherine was worried about Billy, so she was.

## The Adventures of Silly Billy

"Gregory," said his mum. "For the love of the good Lord above and the peace of the neighbourhood, as well as my own sanity, please try to not do anything silly today."

Billy paused for a moment before looking up into the sky, wondering if the good Lord above was going to respond. As she had told him on countless occasions before that she may as well have been talking to the wall, Billy believed his mum must have magical powers. He listened carefully. As he did not hear anything, he continued but was certainly not paying any attention as he closed the garage door behind him.

"Ack, sure aye, ma," said Billy. "I'll be fine. Me and Thunder will be brilliant, so we will. I'll be dead on, I promise."

And with that, while looking back to say goodbye, Billy started up the steep incline of their driveway in first gear only to crash into the gates at the top. He had hoped to show his mum that he could make it onto Knockview Park without having to stop and

## Silly Billy and the Good Deed

get off to push, as Joseph could already do this with ease. He had also wanted to try to show his mum that he was fully aware of his surroundings. What he should have done, however, was to pay close attention as to where he was going although this was much easier said than done. He often found things that easily distracted him which led to one mishap occurring after another. He never learned.

Along with his bike and his schoolbooks which were now emptied out from his bag and lying all over the driveway, Billy lay in a crumpled heap, staring up at the blue sky above with his arm resting on the small, front wheel of his bike. Catherine, who had brought out a bucket of warm, soapy water that morning to wash the windows, looked bewildered at his latest misadventure.

"What on God's green earth have you done now?" she asked.

He dusted himself off and wiped away a few tiny stones that had pressed

## The Adventures of Silly Billy

themselves into his hands while saying, "Tut, Tut, Tut," so that his mum would not have to do so. She already was.

"I was so busy saying goodbye to you, I did not see that the gates were still closed from last night. I thought that maybe you had opened them to take the motor car out so you could bring Karen and Joseph to school? How was I to know they weren't opened."

"Aye, I see that," said his mum. "It would have been better if you would have listened to what I had told you to do this morning. You need to dig the spuds out of your ears. Better yet, open your eyes as well. For Heaven's sakes, if I've told you once..."

"Ack, I know ma... You've told me a thousand times, so you have."

Billy mouthed the words quietly under his breath, though, as he did not want to get in trouble a second time. He often wondered how his mum had managed to keep track of all the times she had told

## Silly Billy and the Good Deed

him before and when that number might actually reach two thousand.

Billy was so excited to take Thunder to school he had forgotten that it was him who had closed the gates the night before. He was trying to do a good deed for his mum in the hopes that he would get some pocket money, as well as her writing a letter to tell his dad all about how good he had been lately.

Unfortunately, for Billy, he was not listening that morning when his mum had reminded him to open the gates before leaving for school. He was far too busy sneaking a peek at a Beano which had come the day before. It was always a race between Billy and his siblings as to who would get the first read. Usually, the one who won was whoever was at home sick the day it arrived, on Wednesday's, when their granny, Mary, would come over with a bottle of Lucozade and made a cup of granny's sweet tea. This would be loaded with three spoonful's of sugar, and seemed to have the

## The Adventures of Silly Billy

magic effect of curing every illness. It was his brother, Joseph, who was the first to cut out the coupon inside the comic and sent it in to join the 'Dennis The Menace' fan club, and received a 'Gnasher' badge with its googly eyes in the post for his efforts of doing so. Everyone, except Billy's mum, took turns to wear the black, furry badge.

Billy stood up, wiped the rest of the stones from his hands, lifted Thunder up of the ground, and put the kickstand down to support the weight of his bicycle. However, as Thunder was standing on the slope of the driveway, the handlebars turned one way, the kickstand gave out, and Thunder toppled over once again.

Shaking her head, his mum said, "Tsk tsk tsk tsk tsk... Once a Silly Billy, always a Silly Billy. Again, I've told you a thousand times before that you cannot leave you bicycle standing on the slope of the driveway, as this is what would happen. Do you ever listen to me at all? Heavens above, I may as well be talking to the wall. Here, let me help you."

# Silly Billy and the Good Deed

With that, she took his bicycle down to the front of the garage and onto the pathway where it would be safe and not fall.

As he picked his bag, books, and himself up from the concrete, Billy looked up to the sky, as he would often do in moments like this. Looking back and forth, he listened carefully to see if the Heavens were going to share their thoughts as well as the wall. His mum walked up to the top of the driveway to open the gates for him.

"What are you looking at?" she asked, unaware that he would do this each time.

"Umm, nothing really, ma."

Thinking of a good excuse, Billy said, "I wanted to make sure that I was not going to get rained on while riding to school this morning."

"Ack, your head's cut, so it is," was her response, as there wasn't a cloud to be seen. Billy wanted to get a move on as he had embarrassed himself enough already.

## The Adventures of Silly Billy

"Right, ma," he shouted, "I'm away now, so I am," and without paying attention, went to kick the kickstand into position, completely missed, and ended up slamming his left shin into the pedal. A large crash followed by a bang, Billy and Thunder fell into the garage door.

**"YEE-OUCH."**

Billy cried out in pain and as he danced around while holding his shin, his books fell out of his school bag since he forgot to buckle the corded straps shut. Everything was in a state of chaos, including Billy, who was obviously not having a good start to his day.

Their next-door neighbour, Mrs. McComish, was out brushing the path along the front of her house and called over asking if everything was okay. Her son, Iain, and Billy, would regularly get together after school and on the weekends to play games on the front street including Kerby and Red Rover. Billy was sure that she too, had eyes on the back of her head. Iain and

## Silly Billy and the Good Deed

Billy would often compare notes about the special and magical powers that both of their mothers seemed to have.

Hearing him yell out, Billy's mum turned to her neighbour and said, "Anne, you know what our boys are like," who responded with, "Sure, our Iain's just as bad. You can't tell him nothing and may as well be speaking to the wall, so you may."

"Aye, I know," said Catherine, turning her attention back to her son.

"Good grief. You'd wake the dead making all that racket, so you would. What did you do now, you Silly Billy?" You really need to be careful. For the love of God and mercy, pay more attention, will ya?"

Grimacing, while holding his shin and waiting for the pain to go away, Billy explained through gritted teeth the latest incident to his mum and his neighbour.

"Sure aye, ma, I will," said Billy. He lifted his trouser leg only to see that he had scraped his shin against the pedal. Even

# The Adventures of Silly Billy

though it was red and stung, Billy hoped that he would forget about it once he began to ride his way to school.

Determined to get a move on, he picked Thunder up off the driveway and started to pedal hard but with his leg still stinging, Billy jumped off halfway up, pulled the left brake lever to help keep his balance, and pushed his bicycle the rest of the way past the gates and onto the footpath outside of their house.

Before getting back on, Billy turned to wish Mrs. McComish a good morning. He asked if Iain had already left for school or if he wanted to perhaps cycle part of the way with him, as his school was over in Mossley, not far from Billy's. He had known Anne his entire life, as she and her husband, Andrew, had bought their house shortly after his mum and dad had bought theirs a few years before Billy was born.

"Iain's off from school sick today, so he is. He has a wee bit of a temperature

## Silly Billy and the Good Deed

and an upset tummy," said Mrs. McComish. "Hopefully, he'll be feeling better after you get home."

"I hope so too," said Billy, "as we were supposed to finish our game of Kerby from yesterday, so we were. I think Iain is winning three games to two right now." Catherine interrupted the conversation.

"I'll Kerby ya, so I will. You had better hurry up and get on to school. You're already behind in your time. Now, go on with ya."

Billy knew his mum was starting to become cross with him as he was stalling for more time.

"Alright ma, see you later," said Billy before speaking to Anne again. "Tell Iain to drink granny's sweet tea as well as have some Lucozade. Oh, and tell him to eat cream of chicken soup, the heel from Mother's Pride bread, and to read the Beano as well. That always makes me feel much better, so it does."

## The Adventures of Silly Billy

What Billy did not explain though is that he wanted to make sure that Iain would be well enough after he got home from school so that they could go back outside and play their game of Kerby instead of doing their homework.

Billy made sure that his foot was properly on the pedal this time and started to push off. Success. Or so he thought. He did not notice that he had accidentally bumped Thunder into third gear. Since it was so much harder to pedal, he got back off Thunder so that he could get his bicycle into the easiest gear.

"Quit messin' about, will ya," said his mum. "What are you up to now? You're puttin' my head away now, so you are. C'mon, I'm going to drive you to school."

She turned to Anne to say cheerio, as she would need to get her coat on and her car keys.

He tried to plead his case as to why he should ride to school. But, before he could,

## Silly Billy and the Good Deed

his mum already starting to share her thoughts.

"Look. Only a Silly Billy could make as many mistakes as you have this morning already and you haven't even left the front of the house yet, so you haven't. One of these days I'm going to pack my bags, run away from you lot of you, and give my head peace."

Not understanding that he and his siblings were quite often the cause of her frustration, Billy provided his usual response when he would hear his mum make such a statement.

"Don't worry mum, I will pack my bags too and come with you."

Determined to get going, Billy put the kickstand back onto the ground, turned the pedal with his hand, put Thunder into first gear, and climbed back on. He looked all around him to make sure that nothing else would happen, double, and triple checked. Everything seemed to be in order.

# The Adventures of Silly Billy

"Right, here I go," said Billy and with that, he was finally off and on his way to school, much to the relief of his mum.

Billy chose to not cycle on the roads today. With all the mishaps he had created that morning, he felt that he would be much safer sticking to the footpaths. Just as he had always found with walking up the steep hill of Knockview Park, he knew that he would only get part way up the street, past house number twelve before he would have to jump off and start pushing.

With his heavy schoolbag on the back carrier of Thunder, this presented to be a bit more of a challenge than he had expected. He looked back at his mum and Anne, who seemed to have stopped talking to closely watch him as he struggled to make his way up the street.

"I'm fine," shouted Billy, and with that, he kept pushing his bicycle.

Once he made it past his Aunty May's house near the top of Knockview Park the

## Silly Billy and the Good Deed

incline was a lot less challenging, so Billy got back on and started slowly pedalling again while trying to pull a few small wheelies as this always seemed to help in getting him going.

Billy reached Knockview Road, dismounted, and while using his Green Cross Code skills that he had learned at school, he crossed over onto Knockview Avenue. He noticed that Mrs. Graham was sitting in her favourite rocking chair where he would normally see her each time he went past her house. Before getting back onto his bicycle, Billy took the time to wave, and gave her a huge smile as well. Although Mr. Graham was not working in his garden, Billy felt that he would see him in the afternoon as he often did after he was done with school.

As the first half of this street was quite flat, Billy managed to get Thunder into second gear and built up a bit of speed to help him get halfway up the steep hill on Knockview Avenue. He figured that this time and with how fast he was going, he

## The Adventures of Silly Billy

would be able to make it to the top and so he moved Thunder into third gear.

He began to ride up the incline without any problems but soon noticed that a car was parked on most of the footpath outside number fourteen. Knowing how clumsy he could be at the best of times, there was no way that he could cycle past it without causing any damage as the car did not leave him enough room. With that, he pulled the brake, skidded, and left a black tyre mark along the edge of the footpath.

After getting off his bike and checking to see if the road was clear of other cars, he walked Thunder around the obstacle and got back onto the footpath. Once again, he would have to put Thunder back into first gear to get to the top of this hill. With that, he decided to push past the remaining two houses on this part of the street and up towards Knockview Gardens where he would have to cross the street to the other side. Billy was starting to wonder if he had made a good choice on wanting to bring his prized bicycle to school due to all of the problems that he had already faced.

    Luckily for him, the journey from that point forward was far less eventful and stressful than what Billy had already experienced throughout the morning. He made his way to the Woodford Road, and crossed over to the Woodford shops. Before following the footpath along Woodford Avenue, he stopped to look at the big, red letterbox. Billy remembered his busy adventure when he had been asked to buy a postage stamp for his mum and post a letter to his dad at sea. What should have perhaps only taken him twenty minutes ended up taking several hours to complete as a result of him making several mistakes along the way. This was not an uncommon occurrence for him.

    After leaving the letterbox, Billy knew that if he stayed on the right footpath, he would not have to stop to use his Green Cross Code instructions until he reached Woodford Park. Once on the other side, he would have to go through the entryway that connected the Woodford district to the Christine area and onto his school.

Making his way through the entry, Billy could quite easily stay on the footpath that ran alongside of Christine Road. Since the trip was going much more smoothly now, he began to feel excited about taking Thunder to school as he knew the other children would ask him about his very cool, purple bicycle with the three gears; the large wheel on the back with the small wheel on the front, along with the chopper style handlebars.

Crossing through the blue iron gates at the top of the entrance to St. MacNissi's primary school, he noticed a group of his classmates were playing football in the playground. Each morning, a captain for each team would be selected, who would then pick their players and have them line up before the game started. Billy would often play the left defender position.

## Silly Billy and the Good Deed

Billy felt very proud when a few of them looked over, seen him on his bike, and began chasing after him towards the front of the school. Unfortunately, for one of the teams playing, this led to a game-winning goal as Michael, who chose himself as the captain to be the goalkeeper, had abandoned his net to chase after Billy. Quite often, the nets were made by children who would place their coats on the dusty playground. They would have to go back to fetch them after the game was done and would go to school looking filthy.

Upon reaching the front doors, he pulled the rear brake a little too hard and noticed that his back tyre had left a BIG, black skid mark.

"Oh no," said Billy. "What have I done? I hope Tommy the Caretaker doesn't get upset with me for that."

He had heard Tommy telling other children before to not leave skid marks from their tyres on the white tile concrete

# The Adventures of Silly Billy

as it made a mess and was difficult for him to clean up.

Billy put the kickstand down, reached into his pocket, and took out his key that he would use to put his blue lock on the back tyre and attach it to the pole. He wanted to make sure that Thunder was safe while he was in school, and so that no other children would try to take his most prized possession for a ride around the playground as they would probably try their best to break it.

A group of his classmates gathered around. Some sat on the seat, asking if they could take Thunder for a ride. Others pulled the brakes, or grabbed the gearbox and moved the lever from first gear to third gear and then to second gear. As they began doing this recklessly, Billy was afraid they were going to break something and started to think once again that it was not such a good idea to bring his bicycle to school after all.

## Silly Billy and the Good Deed

"No, sorry, I can't," said Billy as he pulled his school bag from the back carrier and over his shoulder. "My mum doesn't want anyone on my bike. Anyway, we have to get into class right now, as the bell just rang."

Billy did not like to disappoint people, but also did not want others touching his bicycle.

He began walking towards the front door of his school with his classmates but stopped, went back to where his bicycle was sitting, petted the seat as if it were an animal, and whispered to it.

"Okay Thunder. You wait here for me. Once school is over, we can ride back home again only this time I will get you into third gear as we go down the hills on Knockview Avenue and Knockview Park. It will be great fun and dead fast, so it will."

Billy made his way back into school and upstairs to the second level. He was very proud to be up here as his sister, Karen, and brother, Joseph, were on this same

## The Adventures of Silly Billy

level. As they were older than him, they were in different classrooms than him.

That morning, he worked on his math, reading, and English lessons, and did a spelling test. At break time, he went out to check on his prized bicycle, which was still sitting in the same place where Billy had left it before going into class.

"It'll not be long now, Thunder, before we're riding home again," said Billy. He hoped Iain would be reading the Beano by now, eating his chicken soup, and having a glass of Lucozade or his granny's sweet tea so that they could finish their game of Kerby once he got home and trying to avoid any homework that he would be given.

While the morning dragged on, home time could not come fast enough for Billy, as he always preferred to be out playing with his friends and at home rather than being at school. The reason for this is that one teacher had not been very nice to Billy or his classmates in all his years of going to St. MacNissi's. She was very stern, rude,

## Silly Billy and the Good Deed

or angry with him along with some of his classmates. Billy could not understand why this teacher took his older sister, Karen, and another student, Rachael, out for swimming lessons each week.

This same teacher liked his older brother, Joseph, and would tell their mum that she enjoyed teaching both of his siblings, as they were "very bright and wonderful children." The other kids would call her "Ma Meanie." She was an overgrown bully, and would punish children using a leather strap that she had affectionately named Charlie. Billy avoided her as often as he could since she constantly lived up to her nickname. She would target him regularly and other children within his classroom including a very nice and helpful girl called Gráinne.

At lunchtime, after he had finished eating his cheese triangle, sandwich, and chocolate covered biscuit, he went out to check on Thunder. Miss Sturrock, his primary three teacher, approached Billy and

## The Adventures of Silly Billy

asked if he would go to the local shop for her. He jumped at this chance, as he knew it would be sooner than later that he would get to ride his bike again.

"Ack aye, sure thing," replied Billy excitedly. "I'd love to go and will get my coat on me right away, so I will. I'll leave my school bag here. What do you need me to get for you?"

Miss Sturrock knew that Billy was always keen to complete any task that was given to him, so she asked if he could pick her up five of her favourite sweeties - chocolate coated Highland toffee bars. They cost five pence each but as the school tuck shop did not have any left since the teachers would buy them and the kids who were working in the tuck shop would eat them after the door was closed from break, she gave Billy a fifty pence piece and said that he too could get some for doing a good deed for her. She asked that he go around to the Manse Road Filling Station, as this was the closest

## Silly Billy and the Good Deed

shop to his school and would take no more than ten minutes to complete.

Brimming with excitement, Billy said that he would be back in no time at all. Miss Sturrock thanked him and went back inside to the staff room. Billy, however, changed his mind but did not let her know what his new plan was.

"If I go to the Woodford Shops instead, then I will get a longer ride on Thunder and no one will be any the wiser, so they won't," he thought to himself. As he laughed at this idea, he said, "I'm not Silly Billy. I'm a BRILLIANT Billy!"

With that, he decided to sing a wee song to himself. As he often did, Billy thought that he would sing "The Belle of Belfast City." He had been taught this famous song with his classmates for them to perform in front of their parents at the Christmas school play. However, he always changed the words to something quite different...

# The Adventures of Silly Billy

"I'll tell me ma, when I get home, I went to the shops all on my own. I took my bike and pedalled there, the wind blew around my scruffy hair. I am Silly, I am Billy, I am the King of Belfast City. Without my horse, I'm two foot three; my favourite food is a chip butty."

Since he was so excited about his big idea to get in a longer bike ride and while laughing at himself for changing the words to the famous Belfast song yet again, he jumped onto his bicycle, pushed back the kickstand with his left foot and tried to pedal.

**CRASH. BANG.**

Along with Thunder, Billy fell onto the ground.

**"YEE-OUCH!"** he yelled.

In his haste, Billy had completely forgotten to take the blue lock off from his back tyre. Tommy, who was the school's Caretaker, was just about to leave in his car when he had seen Billy fall to the ground and went over to help him.

## Silly Billy and the Good Deed

"Are you okay, you Silly Billy?" asked Tommy. "Here, let me help you get up."

As Tommy helped Billy, he noticed that there was a **BIG, black skid mark** on the white tile concrete and asked, "Do you know who might have done this, Billy? That wasn't there when I came in this morning and I didn't see your bike here either..."

Tommy gave Billy a look as if he knew who the culprit was, just like his mum would do when she knew that Billy had been up to no good. Billy felt that Tommy also had eyes on the back of his head, just like his mum did and knew who was responsible.

"I think I'm okay," said Billy. He avoided making eye contact with Tommy and did not answer the question that was asked of him.

"Sorry, but I can't wait around. I have to do a good deed for Miss Sturrock and need to get going. She said that it would take about ten minutes. I do not want to disappoint her." Tommy would often give the children who stayed behind after

## The Adventures of Silly Billy

dinner to help him stack chairs a ten pence piece each. The kids felt that they were rich and would spend the money in the tuck shop the next day.

In fact, what Billy did not want Tommy to know was his secret plan of going to a different shop. He picked his bicycle up and put the kickstand back down onto the ground. Reaching into his pocket, he took out his key, removed the lock from his back tyre, attached it to the handlebars, and sat back down on his bicycle. This time, he pushed the pedal downwards as to not bang his shin, kicked back the kickstand, found his footing, checked the gear box to make sure it was in first after his schoolmates had moved the level earlier that morning, and after 'revving the engine', off he went.

A couple of his schoolmates were playing football and shouted over to him as he cycled past them.

"Hey Billy," they asked. "Where are you off too? Do you want to join us? We need another defender, so we do."

## Silly Billy and the Good Deed

    This time, he pulled on the brake lever carefully to tell them that he had an important job to do for Miss Sturrock, and would be back in no time at all. Even though he had stopped for only a few seconds, Billy did not want to waste any time. With all of his might, he pulled a wheelie further than what he had wanted too, which made the small front wheel go straight up into the air with Billy having to jump off and land on his two feet. Although this looked like it was a pretty spectacular stunt, he knew that he was wasting more time. He continued on but pulled a few more, smaller wheelies.

    After he got outside of the blue, iron gates of St. MacNissi's, Billy looked back to check and make sure that no one was watching him go in the opposite direction from that of where he was supposed to go, which was to the right towards the Manse Road Filling Station. Instead, Billy followed the same pathways that he took that morning while coming to school and arrived at the entryway in no time at all. However, someone had dropped a milk bottle within

# The Adventures of Silly Billy

the entry itself, which meant that there was now a pile of broken glass scattered all over the ground. Billy slowed down to avoid the glass, as he did not want to get a puncture in his tyre since he would have to ask his brother to help him fix it. Joseph was always really good at fixing things, and would use spoons from their mum's kitchen drawer to take the tyre off of the wheel before using the puncture repair kit to fix it. No matter how often Billy tried to fix his own punctures, he was never as good as Joseph, and would often end up with cuts, scrapes, and bruises all over his hands.

    At the other side of the entry, Billy stopped to cross Woodford Park. There was a lot more traffic, so he waited until it was safe to cross and made his way over. He pedalled as slowly as he could along the footpath, as he wanted to take his time and enjoy his bike ride before eventually pulling into the Woodford Shops. He did not use his lock.

## Silly Billy and the Good Deed

Upon seeing Billy, the shopkeeper, Aubrey, asked him why he was out of school.

Excited to tell Aubrey and while placing the fifty pence on the counter, Billy said, "I need five chocolate-coated Highland toffee bars for Miss Sturrock. She sent me to do a good deed for her and for that I am allowed to get some of the same sweets."

"Well, that is awfully nice of you, Billy," replied Aubrey. "But I am very sorry to let you know that you are five minutes too late. I sold the last of them to another customer."

Billy thought about how could he have missed out on being at the shops five minutes sooner but realized he had forgotten to take the lock from his bike, crashed, and that the broken glass in the entryway had slowed him down. Also, he was told to go to the shop closest to his school and if he had followed the instructions that Miss Sturrock had given to him in the first place, he wouldn't be out of luck. He could hear his mum's voice ringing in his head,

# The Adventures of Silly Billy

saying, "Billy, if I've told you once, I've told you a thousand times..."

"Why didn't I just do as I was asked," said Billy to himself in a quiet voice. "I am sure if Miss Sturrock finds out what I've done, she'll tell me ma. I'll be in big trouble when I get home. Then my ma will tell my da about it in one of the letters she sends to him at sea, and he'll be cross with me when he gets home for not listening as he always brings those letters with him in his suitcase, so he does. I'm doomed. Unless my ma gets me to bring that letter to the post office and I don't post it but throw it away instead."

Billy realized the more that he planned to try and cover up what he had done wrong, the more trouble he was going to get himself into. Not to be beaten, changing his mind, and hoping to fix his mistake by completing the good deed that he was asked to do, Billy smiled and said, "No problem, Aubrey, If I go around to the

## Silly Billy and the Good Deed

Manse Road Filling Station, I bet they have lots. I can buy them there."

"That is a great idea," replied Aubrey as he gave him back the fifty pence. "Good luck, make sure and certain to be careful. Watch the road for cars, mind yourself well."

Billy thanked him and out the door he went. Although the direction to his house was straight ahead of him and while he stared up at the Knockagh Monument in the distance on the mountaintop directly behind his house, he knew his mum would be very upset if he went there due to all of the mistakes that he had made that morning and not getting off to school on time. He decided to go the way that he had told Aubrey.

Once again, while following the footpath along Woodford Avenue, Billy pedalled as hard and as fast as he could as to not have another five minutes beat him out of getting his own sweets. The muscles in his legs burned since he had kept Thunder in first gear. As he had built up enough speed though, he was able to freewheel for a

## The Adventures of Silly Billy

bit and in no time at all, was back at the Woodford Road and crossed over.

Since he was in such a hurry, he had completely forgotten that a glass bottle had been broken. In trying to avoid the sharp pieces, he lost his balance and crashed into a wooden fence that had just been freshly stained on one side of the entryway. The smell from the stain was very strong and filled the air, including his nostrils.

Checking to make sure there was no damage and in seeing that his tyres did not get punctured, Billy continued out onto the Christine Road and over to Christine Drive. He pedalled furiously to get to the end of this street, onto Christine Park, which would then lead him across a small field and over to the Manse Road Filling Station. He felt much better and although he was completely out of breath, he opened the door of the shop and went up to the counter where all of the sweets were kept.

The shopkeeper had noticed that Billy was frantically scanning the layers of

## Silly Billy and the Good Deed

shelves and their sweets back and forth. Finally, he asked, "Is there something that I can help you to find, son?"

While panting, Billy explained in gasps to the shopkeeper the good deed that he had been given by his teacher, but could not find the items he was looking for: bars of chocolate covered Highland toffee.

"Oh, I am sorry," said the shopkeeper, "but it seems those are very popular. I sold the last of them about five minutes ago to another fellow who came in to get some petrol. If you had of been here a wee bit faster, I would have had some for you no problem. I'll have to put an order in to my supplier to get some more, so I will, but that won't be for a few days yet. Maybe you can come back then."

Disappointed and while hanging his head, Billy remembered to use his manners and thanked the shopkeeper. As he walked out to Thunder, he said, "Now what? If only I came here first and not rode around to the Woodford Shops, I would have our

## The Adventures of Silly Billy

sweets by now. I can't go back to the school without them."

Billy sat for a moment on the seat of his bicycle before realizing that he could go to the Beverly shops, which were just around the corner from the Filling Station. He was not aware of how much time he had already wasted by going to two places which were in complete opposite directions of one another.

"I bet they have them there, they always have loads of everything."

Without giving it a second thought, he set off along the footpath beside the Manse Road and up towards the Beverly area.

Billy stopped at Glenkyle Park and followed his Green Cross Code training. He was extra careful though, as the Manse Road was very busy with lots of cars and lorries, as well as pedestrians walking along the footpaths since there was a school just across the street called Mossley, which is the same one that Iain went too. He wanted

## Silly Billy and the Good Deed

to make sure that he looked all directions before crossing.

Upon reaching the other side, he got back onto his bike and started pedalling as fast as he could. His legs ached but as he did not like to disappoint anyone, he was determined to complete this very important job for Miss Sturrock.

At last, he reached the Beverly Road. This had a slight incline to it but would take him up to the Beverly Shops. Billy was determined to cycle up this road without having to get off his bike. He put Thunder into first gear and using every ounce of strength that his legs had even though they felt like jelly from pedalling so hard, he continued.

Once he reached the Mace and since he was not as familiar with this area as he was with Knockview and Woodford, he took the blue lock from his handlebars, placed Thunder up against a steel fence, and placed the lock around the large, back wheel. He went into the shop and just as

## The Adventures of Silly Billy

he had done at the Filling Station, began to frantically search the shelves.

At last, Billy saw the box he was looking for. Reaching in, he found that it had more than enough! Excited, he grabbed a bunch only to find that they were not the chocolate covered kind but instead, were just the regular bars. Someone had put them there by mistake. Billy could not believe what he was seeing and took the box down to have a look to see if there were other bars. There weren't any to be found.

"Oh no, not again," sighed Billy. "Now what am I going to do?" I've been to three places, so I have, and none of them have chocolate covered Highland toffee. Of all the rotten luck in the world..."

Hanging his head while walking out of the shops towards his bike, Billy realized that there was at least one more shop to go to at the top of the Carnmoney Road. However, he would probably have to push Thunder all the way up an extremely steep hill that he knew would not only leave him

## Silly Billy and the Good Deed

breathless and his legs completely weak, he likely would not have any strength left to cycle back. Billy thought to himself that he should give up, go back to school, disappoint his teacher by telling her what he had done wrong in the first place, and get into trouble for not listening to what she had asked him to do.

"No," said Billy while taking the blue lock off of Thunder's back wheel. "We can do this, we are going to do this, and we're not going back to school until we have the bars. This is our chance to make things right, so it is. I have to make things right."

Billy groaned and then let out a huge sigh of disappointment. "If only I had of listened the first time around I would have already done my good deed and would have some sweets to eat." He was quite upset with himself. Just as his mum had always said, once Billy got an idea into his head, it was hard to make him change his mind as he was determined to get things done. She often would call this as being 'bull headed.'

# The Adventures of Silly Billy

Billy crossed the Beverly Road and pulled Thunder up onto the footpath on the other side. He knew that he would have to cross five streets before reaching the shop at the top of the Carnmoney Road called Helen's and Alan's. Taking a deep breath, he set off once again.

By far, this was one of the most difficult bicycle rides that Billy had ever done. As he made his way up the road, Billy thought that riding up his own street of Knockview Park and that of Knockview Avenue was the easiest thing he could do. However, no matter how hard he tried, there was just no way that he could ride up this road. The hill was far too steep.

Billy dismounted his bicycle and walked while pushing it alongside of him. Huffing and puffing, he stopped every so often and watched as cars zoomed past without any effort at all, or so it seemed.

He had become so consumed by all the cars passing him that he did not realize just how far he had walked and pushed Thunder.

## Silly Billy and the Good Deed

He had already crossed four of the five streets safely. All he had to do now was to cross the top of the Ballyduff Road and at last, he would be at Helen's and Alan's wee shop. Determined to make it and with renewed strength in his legs, he continued.

Billy used his Green Cross Code and crossed the one last road to the shop. A smile burst upon his face as he thought to himself, "Yes. I did it. I made it." He looked behind him and could see his own district in the distance along with the Knockagh Monument, which he could see clearly up on the side of the mountain directly behind his house on Knockview Park. It was so much further away from when he looked at it while standing outside of the Woodford Shops.

"Wow," he gasped. "Look how far I've gone to complete this job I was given by my teacher." Just wait until I tell my classmates about this adventure and how far I had to go to get her some sweeties." Billy felt like he was on top of the world.

# The Adventures of Silly Billy

Proudly, yet exhausted, he made the last steps he needed to go to lock up his bike to the fence and in he went. Just as he had done at each of the other shops, he looked high and low at the shelves to find the treasure he had been seeking. Things did not look promising.

"You've got to be kidding me," he shrieked when he did not see any. He looked again but there was nothing. Not even a box this time with the wrong kind of bar in it, but an empty space where the box of sweets should have been. He began looking at shelves of groceries only to be met with further disappointment. Billy's face became flush red as if he was going to erupt like a volcano about to blow its top.

"DO YOU MEAN TO TELL ME THAT I WENT TO FOUR SHOPS TO DO A GOOD DEED, AND THAT I HAD TO PUSH MY BIKE ALL THE WAY UP THE CARNMONEY ROAD ONLY TO NOW FIND OUT THAT NO ONE HAS A

## Silly Billy and the Good Deed

**BAR OF CHOCOLATE COVERED HIGHLAND TOFFEE. THAT'S NOT FAIR, SO IT'S NOT!"**

Billy did not realize that he was now shouting at the top of his lungs. The shopkeeper, who was in the back getting some supplies, came out to ask what the fuss was about.

"Hey, would you please keep it down, you Silly Billy," said the shopkeeper, who did not know that this was what people would call him on a regular basis. "Are you trying to scare away my customers? You'd wake the dead with all that racket you're making, so you would." Billy did not realize how loud his voice was.

"I'm sorry," said Billy, and went on to explain how he had gone to the Woodford Shops only to be five minutes too late; that he then went to the Manse Road Filling Station where he was supposed to go only to be five minutes too late; that he then went to the Beverly Shops only to find they had regular toffee in the box and now,

## The Adventures of Silly Billy

after walking his way up the extremely steep Carnmoney Road all the while pushing his bike the entire time, to find that the shop here had none either and that his teacher would be extremely disappointed because he didn't do as he was told in the first place.

"Okay, take a breath, wee lad," said the shopkeeper. "It must be your lucky day. I ordered new stock in and you are the first person to ask for them. How many would you like?"

Billy took the fifty pence out of his pocket and at first thought about how many he could have for himself and could eat before he got back to school. He decided to shout out his answer so that the good Lord above would also hear him.

"I WILL BUY TEN CHOCOLATE COVERED HIGHLAND TOFFEE. FIVE FOR MY TEACHER, MISS STURROCK, ONE FOR MY MUM, ONE FOR MY SISTER, KAREN, ONE FOR MY BROTHER, JOSEPH,

# Silly Billy and the Good Deed

**ONE FOR MY WEE SISTER, ANGELA, AND OF COURSE I WILL HAVE ONE MYSELF FOR ALL MY HARD WORK ALTHOUGH I DESERVE THEM ALL SINCE I WORKED SO HARD TO FIND THESE FOR MY TEACHER TO BEGIN WITH..."**

Billy then lowered his voice and said, "That way, I also won't get into any trouble."

The shopkeeper chuckled and told Billy that there was no need to shout. He counted out ten bars, and put five each into two separate paper bags so that he could give one bag to his teacher, while the other bag would go home with him at the end of the day after school.

After collecting the money from Billy, the shopkeeper said:

> "Good luck and be careful. That is very nice that you are going to share with your family. But, you should share from your heart and

## The Adventures of Silly Billy

not because you do not want to get into trouble for not following the instructions your teacher gave you in the first place. Now, please watch the road for cars and enjoy your sweets. Your teacher will be quite happy with your good deed as you have certainly put a lot of hard work into it after realizing the mistake you made to begin with. I hope you learned a very valuable lesson today, young lad."

Billy nodded his head, thanked the shopkeeper, and left. As he unlocked Thunder, he said, "Now we have to make our way back and it is all downhill from here. We probably will not even need to use the third gear, but I don't know if I will make it all the way back to my school. I've no energy left."

Billy was right. In fact, he did not need to use any gear. As he picked up so much speed from going down the extremely steep hill, he needed his brakes now more than

## Silly Billy and the Good Deed

anything. Using his Green Cross Code and in no time at all, he was back at the bottom of the Carnmoney road, onto the Beverly Road, over to the Manse Road past the Filling Station, and on toward the Christine Road. Billy realized he had barely pedalled at all since everything was downhill from Helen's and Alan's shop and so cycling back to his school from this point seemed easy.

As Billy pulled Thunder back through the blue iron gates at the top of St. MacNissi's primary school, he was surprised to see that there were no children outside playing.

"Where did everyone go?" he thought to himself. "Did I miss something? I bet they are all hiding on me inside the school."

Billy went back to the front of the school and locked up his bicycle.

"There we go, Thunder," he said. "We did it. We made it. You did it. My teacher will be so proud of me, so she will. I will be her favourite student from now on."

# The Adventures of Silly Billy

Walking into the school, Billy was further surprised to see that there were no kids in the hallways. He made his way up the stairs to the second level and walked into the classroom where all the children were seated. Miss Sturrock's face turned pure white as if she had seen a ghost, but then looked both relieved and shocked to see Billy.

"Where have you been?" she asked with a very cross and stern voice. "We have been looking everywhere for you. We had even contacted your mum, as we thought you might have gone home."

Billy's smile quickly faded away as he knew what was coming next.

"Your mum told us that when you are given a task or are asked to do something, you don't stop until you have completed it. What did she call it? Oh, right. Bull headed! What I want to know right now though is this. What happened? Did you get hurt? Where did you go? Are you okay? I will have to let Mr. Herron know that you made it back."

## Silly Billy and the Good Deed

Mr. Herron, the school principal, had seen that Billy's bicycle was locked up outside and appeared in the classroom just as his teacher had finished asking where he was.

Billy took the time to recall everywhere he had been and what he had to do to find the five, chocolate covered Highland toffee bars for his teacher. He did not realize, however, that he had been gone for almost **two hours**. After he explained himself, Billy took out one of the bags that contained the sweets from his coat pocket and handed them to his teacher.

"Here you go, Miss Sturrock," he announced while glancing at Mr. Herron, who did not look very happy at all with what he had done. Billy hoped that this would get him out of the trouble he had now created for himself, but was also secretly happy that he was out of school for that long.

"Thank you, Gregory, for going to all that effort in getting those," said Miss Sturrock. Since his teacher had used his real name like his mum would do when she

## The Adventures of Silly Billy

was upset with him and had not called him by his nickname, he felt that there was a lot of trouble awaiting him. She continued to share her thoughts.

"But, do you see the next time, if there is a next time and if I ask you to go to the shop for me, you are to please follow the instructions that I gave you to do in the first place. And, if they don't have the items I ask you to get, you are to come straight back to the school. Everyone was so worried about you, including your mum. Mr. Herron, can you please call Catherine and let her know that Gregory is now back safe and sound. Thank you."

Turning to the classroom, she said, "Let this be a lesson to everyone about following instructions and not doing your own thing. Thankfully, nothing happened."

He sighed while his cheeks turned a bright shade of red. Several thoughts ran through his mind of what kind of trouble he was in. He began wondering what his ma was going to say when he got home. Would she be

## Silly Billy and the Good Deed

upset that he did his own thing and did not do what his teacher had asked him to do in the first place? Would she be upset that he missed almost two hours of school? Would she be upset that a teacher had to call her to ask where he was even though he was trying to do a good deed? Would she write a special letter to his dad to tell him about this and the problems it caused and how his classmates learned a lesson at his expense? Would she not let him post the letter since he couldn't even do that properly?

Just then, Tommy stopped by the classroom. He knocked on the door, popped his head in, and nodded to all the students that had been sitting in silence but were now staring at him instead of Billy.

"Sorry to interrupt, Miss Sturrock," he stated. "While I was out getting some supplies for the tuck shop here at the school, I stopped by the Woodford shops and picked you up some of your favourite sweets - chocolate covered Highland toffee. Would you believe how lucky I was,

## The Adventures of Silly Billy

as there were only five bars left inside of the box. I bought them all, so I did."

Billy's eyes widened. He could not believe what he was hearing and realized that the person who bought the last of these sweets five minutes before he got there was the school caretaker.

Before he could open his mouth to ask why, he began thinking about how he had been a Silly Billy and by trying to rush to do his good deed, he had forgotten to take the lock off the back wheel of his bicycle which caused him to crash; how he stopped to talk to his friends who were playing a game of football to tell them about the important job he had to do, and how a milk bottle was broken in the entryway which slowed him down. He thought that if only he had gone the Manse Road Filling Station in the first place as he had been asked to do, he would have completed his important job and would have been back to the school much sooner to also play football with his friends after lunch.

## Silly Billy and the Good Deed

His cheeks turned a bright shade of red once more. It seemed that Billy had learned a very valuable lesson, so he decided not to ask after all. At that moment, he thought that he would rather not eat sweets ever again and pulled his head into his sweater like a turtle would with its shell.

Tommy continued. "Oh, and by the way, Miss Sturrock. I had to go by the Filling Station on the Manse Road to get some petrol for my car and air in the tyres. While I was there, I saw that they too only had five bars of chocolate covered Highland toffee left, and since the Beverly Shops were out of them, I scooped them up."

Looking directly at Billy, he winked and said, "That way, we have a few extra bars on hand to share with our wonderful pupils when they go out of their way to do a good deed..."

# The Adventures of Silly Billy

That concludes the story about my Good Deed and trying to find Chocolate Covered Highland Toffee Bars for my teacher. Even though I made an awesome adventure out of it, I did not realize how worried everyone was about me at the time since I was gone for almost two full hours.

My mum was not happy with me and my adventure either. I am sure the letters she wrote to my dad at sea (which I may have posted to him at some point and only after learning that 1) a stamp was needed and 2) it should not be placed upside down on the envelope), that this may have been the reason why I never became the Man of the House.

Looking back now, I guess I made things extremely easy for Mr. Bossy Boots. Like my mum would often say, boys will be boys, but I was definitely a Silly Billy!

## THE END

# Silly Billy and the Good Deed

# The Adventures of Silly Billy

SILLY BILLY and the Escape from Carrick Castle

By Greg McVicker

# Silly Billy and the Escape from Carrick Castle

## Dedication:

This story, **Silly Billy and the Escape from Carrick Castle**, is dedicated to my father, Charles McVicker. We only ever got to see my dad for approximately two weeks out of every year, since he spent his life at sea due to the troubled times that we grew up with throughout the 1970's and 1980's in Belfast, Northern Ireland.

Whenever he came home, he would always make time to look after his house, but would also take us to see all of the latest Hollywood films, day trips out to the beach at Cushendall, as well as to visit our relatives within Belfast.

This was also before he headed back out to sea, and would work up to an extra 400 hours of overtime per month on top of his regular duties, living on ships, and saving his money to ensure that there was more than enough of a pay packet coming in to keep his kids alive, all the while our dedicated mother, Catherine, continually chased after the ongoing medical needs of four heavily chronic asthmatic children all the while worrying about our safety during one of Ireland's darkest periods of history called 'The Troubles'.

Thank you very much, dad, for creating so many wonderful memories, and for taking us to every movie that you had seen at sea when you came home and would spoil us to bits with sweets, drinks, popcorn, and ice cream, only to then spoil each movie to bits for us by telling us the plot before we had even started the screening.

Lastly, thank you for looking after us all and saving our lives during the bombing that occurred during the James Bond 007 movie "For Your Eyes Only" at the ABC Cinema on Great Victoria Street in Belfast, a day that none of us have forgotten. "Stay down and don't move. You don't go outside, as there might be a second one waiting for you."

**– My love to you, Charles McVicker.**

# The Adventures of Silly Billy

Since it was in the middle of July, Billy did not have school to go to and would spend his time riding his prized possession, his bicycle that he had nicknamed 'Thunder'. Billy loved to take Thunder on many adventures, including when he would cycle up with his older brother, Joseph, to the Knockagh Monument that stood tall on a mountain behind their house. 110 feet tall, to be exact. That was always an awful journey though, since Billy had to cycle up a long and winding road to the top of the mountain.

Even once Billy reached there and though his journey was done, he always forgot that he would have to cycle along another long road before he would reach the entrance road to Knockagh, which was just as steep as the mountain road that he just rode up. Billy was always exhausted after he made the trek and would spend ages at Knockagh trying to catch his breath.

It was his brother, Joseph, who was the first to reach Knockagh before using their

# Silly Billy and the Escape from Carrick Castle

father's binoculars that they brought with them. The first thing that Billy and Joseph would do is to look at the massive size of the Monument which looked very tiny from their home, before looking at their house which was now quite small. They would see their mum, Catherine, out hanging the washing on the clothes line at the back of the home. Although they would shout and scream at the top of their lungs in trying to catch her attention, before jumping up and down so that she could see where their latest adventures had taken them, their mum couldn't hear or see them and would continue with the washing.

    Other things that Billy loved to do during his time off from school was to play in the forest along the Doagh Road, which was just around the corner from his house, or taking his mum's broom to the bottom of their street in Knockview Park. From here, Joseph taught him and their older sister, Karen, how to sweep the stones ahead of them along with the dust from the road, to make tracks which they would try to

# The Adventures of Silly Billy

follow on their bicycles without falling off. Along with Karen, Billy and Joseph spent hours upon hours here having fun. However, Catherine would become upset with them since they would often cycle back to their house and leave her good broom there.

It was Joseph who came to the bottom of the street on this particular morning. He said that since it was a warm and sunny day in Knockview Park, that he and Billy should go fishing instead of doing what they always did, playing on the tracks that they had made the night before. Joseph had just returned from hanging out with all of his friends who lived around the Knockview and Woodford areas, all while riding his own, red, matching Raleigh Chopper. He told Billy about their plan to go fishing down at the marina beside the Carrickfergus Castle and that everyone had gone to get their bicycles. Billy started to think back about what he had learned the last time he had gone there.

# Silly Billy and the Escape from Carrick Castle

It was known to many of the local people as Carrick Castle, and stood on the northern shores of Belfast Lough. This mighty, Norman stronghold was built in the year 1177. The last time Billy had visited Carrick Castle was as a youngster. His teachers at St. MacNissi's had taken Billy and his school mates on a trip there to learn all about the invasions that occurred during that time. Billy remembered looking at the cannon's there, as well as the cannon balls that had been glued together and sat on the ground beside each cannon. He remembered the big portcullis at the front door, and the hole that was directly above it. They were told that boiling tar or water would be poured down on to the invaders below when they became trapped by the portcullis and the wooden doors of the castle.

"Wow!" thought Billy to himself for a moment before responding.

"Fishing? Down at Carrickfergus? Really? Can we fish from the castle? Can we sit on

# The Adventures of Silly Billy

the cannons and catch the fish from there? Perhaps we give the fish we catch to the castle and they can use them on invaders who get stuck in-between the portcullis and the wooden doors, and then be attacked with slimy scales? I love fishing! Let's go!"

It was obvious that Billy had become so caught up in his usual daydreams that he has missed Joseph telling him that they would be fishing from the marina beside Carrick Castle and not from the inside the castle itself. Joseph did not want to remind Billy that the invasions occurred several centuries before, and that fish scales being tossed on to the invaders would likely not be much of a punishment.

Without thinking about being careful, Billy jumped on to Thunder and went to do what he often did, and tried to kick back the kickstand of his bike. Instead, he slammed his shin into the pedal. It is a wonder why Billy never thought of asking his mother to buy him a set of shin guards before trying to go for a bike ride. He had so many bruises along his legs that anyone who saw them would think that Billy was trying to be George Best, Kenny Dalglish, or another world-famous football player who made several tackles only to end up gaining several bruises in the process.

**"OUCH!"**

Billy let out yet another large yelp as his brother looked on and did what their mother, Catherine, did on a regular basis. He stared up towards the heavens above him and shook his head back and forth. Bringing his head back down and after shaking it several more times, he finally spoke.

"Now, listen up, will ye," said Joseph." Ma asked me to bring the broom back up to the house. She doesn't want it left down here like it always happens. The last time she came looking for it she said that she found the broom up in the tree. I know for a fact that I did not leave it there. I always keep it on the footpath to ensure it is safe, so I do."

# The Adventures of Silly Billy

"Aye, that was me," said Billy. "I thought that if I were to brush the bark on the tree, it would help clean all of the dust and the stones of the broom before I brought it home for ma. The only problem with that is that the broom got stuck. I forgot to ask you for your help to get it back, since you are also the best at climbing the tree and putting up our swing, so you are. At least the tree looks clean, so it does."

Again, Joseph shook his head back and forth while making the same "Tut, Tut, Tut," sounds that their mother would also often make while speaking to them.

"Right," he said. "I am away to give ma her broom and will grab our fishing rods. Don't be long. The lads are waiting for us, so they are."

As Joseph turned to take the broom back up to their house which wasn't too far away from the bottom of their street, Billy then busied himself in looking to see what kind of scratches and bruises he earned himself now for being such a silly young

# Silly Billy and the Escape from Carrick Castle

fellow. As was normally the case, Billy's leg had started to go red with a spot of blood appearing at the location where he had scraped the skin off from along his shin. Billy wiped his hand up and down his leg only to make it burn and sting a little bit more. He never learned from all the previous times that he had done this.

Billy was so excited about the thought of going fishing without a grownup and that this was such a great idea, he began daydreaming about all the other times that he had gone fishing before. He thought back to when he first learned how to fish, and the adventures that came with it at the Boghill and Hyde Park dams. He was snapped out of his reflective daydream by his brother, Joseph.

"Oi, you Silly Billy," his brother shouted. "Are we ready to go fishing or what? I've been standing in front of the house now and calling you for ages. I thought that you needed to dig the spuds out of your ears. Did you not hear me? I am sure that I have

## The Adventures of Silly Billy

awoken the dead by now I've been shouting down to you that much."

"Aye, dead on. No worries. Sure, I'm coming now, so I am."

Billy finally made his move towards his brother, while thinking more about the last time he went fishing. Like a lot of Billy's memories, it seemed to him like it was only yesterday. It wasn't.

One day, three years prior and without knowing about it, his uncle Malcolm and his wife, Maureen, who was Billy's aunt and the sister to his mum, Catherine, along with their daughter, Billy's cousin, Treasaigh, all suddenly decided to move back to Canada. They did not go to Nova Scotia as they had done so the first time, but instead settled in a place called Winnipeg. This was where Billy's uncle, John, who was Maureen and Catherine's older brother, also lived with his own family. Billy had never met that side of the family before, but he knew that his mum would write letters and would send

# Silly Billy and the Escape from Carrick Castle

cassette tapes with her voice that she had recorded using a tape recorder to them.

The only other thing that Billy knew about Winnipeg is that it had a lot of flies called mosquitoes. Treasaigh had told Billy that these flies loved to bite people, sucked their blood, and that Winnipeg and Canada had lots and lots of snow. So much snow, that they had snow days and would not be able to go to school. Billy wished that he could get the same snow that Canada gets so that he would not have to go to school ever again, and could instead stay home, make snow castles outside the front of their house with their mum's washing up basin, along with rolling the snow up in the front garden to make snowmen.

Billy then thought about the other thing that Canada had. Nasty flies. And since his older sister, Karen, used to love frightening him and his younger sister, Angela, at night time by telling them spooky stories about ghosts and vampires, as well as showing them scary black and white movies on her

# The Adventures of Silly Billy

television set, Billy thought the mosquitoes had fangs and would fly around in the snow biting people and sucking their blood. Then again, who would want to have snow every day of the year, except for to build snowmen, snow castles, and to have snowball fights while trying to avoid being eaten alive by monstrous, horrible, blood sucking Canadian mosquitoes who lived in Winnipeg.

    Finally, and after arriving at their house, Billy learned that Joseph had grown so impatient with him that he had already dug up the worms that they needed, and had put their fishing rods together. Billy was quite relieved with this, since he did not have to chase birds away who had plucked them out of the wet grass for their breakfast from the rain the night before, or dig for wiggly worms with their dad's garden hand fork tool. The mates Joseph made plans with had already arrived at their house with their own collection of worms and were impatiently waiting for Billy as well.

# Silly Billy and the Escape from Carrick Castle

"Right," said Joseph. "C'mon. It's time we go. If we don't, it'll be nighttime before we get down to Carrickfergus, so it will, and we'll have to make our way straight back. There won't be any time for fishing."

Billy did not want to miss out and immediately grabbed on to his fishing rod. However, and since he was so clumsy, when he tried to copy his older brother by holding his rod in one hand and the handlebars of Thunder with the other, he ended up poking one of his brothers' friends in the back of his head while narrowly missing another. Some of the other fellows laughed in disbelief. They had all been told about how clumsy and silly he was, and here they were now seeing it first hand for themselves.

"Is there anything your brother can do without making a mistake?" said the fellow who was poked in the back of the head, all the while rubbing it. He looked at Billy and continued with his thoughts.

# The Adventures of Silly Billy

"Here, do you see when we get down to Carrickfergus, I want you to go on the other side of the marina and as far away from me so that way I can fish without getting bonked in the head by your rod."

The other fellows laughed at hearing this.

"I will just stay to the back of the line, so I will," muttered Billy as everyone else took their position and started riding their bikes towards the steep slope of Knockview Park. Billy knew that he would likely fall behind the pack as he did not have the strength in his legs to make it all the way up to the top of his street. He tried riding Thunder diagonally, although he knew that it was going to be even more difficult now as he also had his fishing rod in his hand.

The leader of the group chose their route as he had cycled it many times before. Upon reaching the top of Knockview Park, he decided to take a right and followed along the footpath down Knockview Road and over towards the forest on the Doagh Road. Each rider would shout

# Silly Billy and the Escape from Carrick Castle

instructions back to the next to ensure that everyone remained safe.

At the top of the Doagh Road and as they passed over the small concrete railroad bridge, they found themselves now moving on to the same road that Billy and Joseph would take towards the Knockagh Monument before turning onto the long, skinny, winding road that was so difficult to pedal along. Everyone waited for Billy since he seemed to be the slowest rider of them all. As his hands were both tied up in trying to use his handlebars as well as hold on to his fishing rod, he was not able to use the three gears that Thunder had, and would have to stay in one gear only, the easiest. This was great, except that he could not get much speed going and was often well back of the other cyclists.

Waiting to ensure that there were no cars or lorries coming, Billy, Joseph, and his group of mates made their way across and started pedalling along the Old Carrick Road. To the right of them all was the back of the

# The Adventures of Silly Billy

Doagh Road forest, a playground of sorts that had a small stream flowing through it which started at the mill in Mossley and would continue over a waterfall that they all played near when setting up a swing.

As this road was so flat without the challenge of hills, Billy very carefully gripped his fishing rod and the handlebars of Thunder a little tighter while reaching to change the gear into second. As he did, however, he noticed a drain on the side of the curb. Since he didn't want to chance falling off and destroying his rod, let alone giving Thunder yet another puncture which seemed to happen all too often, he lifted his left foot from the pedal and used it to change the gear instead. Billy thought to himself that if anyone could see him doing this, they would think that he was an expert stunt man and was pulling one of his best tricks ever. What Billy did not expect, though, is that he missed the second gear completely and instead pushed Thunder into third gear. Suddenly, it felt like his legs were going to fall off of him since it was

# Silly Billy and the Escape from Carrick Castle

now so much harder to pedal his beloved bike. Billy was glad that none of the other fellows in the group saw this happen.

Grunting and groaning, Billy took his foot from his pedal again and tried to use the back of his heel to knock the gear level back into second. This was so much harder than it looked and did not work. The other problem was that the other riders were starting to break away even further from him as they made their way along the road, eager to get fishing as soon as possible.

Seeing that there was a wide footpath directly ahead of him where he could reset his footing, he stopped pedalling and wheeled Thunder over to it. When he finally came to a stop, Billy found that his hand was cramped and extremely sore when he tried to let go of the handlebar.

Staring at his hand, it reminded him of his Steve Austin bionic man figurine that came with an orange iron bar that he would lift. Steve Austin was dead brilliant, so he was. While pressing the orange button

## The Adventures of Silly Billy

repeatedly that was sticking out of his back and through his red tracksuit, his bionic arm would rise and lift up the iron bar that was actually made of rubber.

Steve Austin also had a bionic eye that Billy could look through from the back of his head, which would make everything look bigger. Billy often wished that he had bionic legs, just like Steve Austin, as he would be able to pedal his bike faster than anyone else, start fishing with his bionic arms, and catch fish that were the size of small boats. Billy also wanted to be a Six Million Dollar Man, although he would have preferred a different colour of tracksuit than the red one that Steve wore all the time.

Suddenly, Billy heard his name being called. One of the fellows that was cycling and who had a ten-speed racer came back to find him, to make sure that he was okay, and that he did not have a flat tyre. Of course, he found Billy to be lost in what else, but another daydream about Steve Austin, the Six Million Dollar Man who was Bionic.

# Silly Billy and the Escape from Carrick Castle

"Billy, you have to try and pay better attention. Everyone is up ahead waiting for you, so they are. Your brother asked me to double back and to check on you. Are you alright? What's causing you to stall the ball?"

Billy explained how his hand had grown tired and cramped because of holding on to his fishing rod and his handlebars all the while trying to change his gears at the same time. He said that he had thought about taking the plastic bag that was lying on the side of the road beside him, and would put his fishing rod in there instead which might make it a little bit easier for him to carry his rod.

"Why didn't you just say something while we were back at your house," was the response that came. "My da has a bag of these things. They are called zip ties. Watch, I will tie your rod to your bike and you will be able to use your gears. Where were you when I was sorting some of the other lads?"

# The Adventures of Silly Billy

Billy ignored the question and asked if he could instead tie his rod to the back carrying frame of Thunder, as that was the place he would always keep his schoolbag. Billy also had another idea in mind though, which he thought would make Thunder look really sleek.

After they finished, Billy reset his gears and his pedals before setting off again along the Old Carrick Road and through the small community of Green Island. Billy looked to his right to see if he could find his house. On the left side and on top of the mountain was the Knockagh Monument. Billy decided he would put his new plan into action.

Pretending that his fishing rod was now an antenna on the back of Thunder, Billy would cycle along so much easier now, changing the gears from first, to second, to third. As he was doing this, he would bring his hand up to his mouth and while speaking into his fist, began pretending that Thunder had a CB radio on it as well.

# Silly Billy and the Escape from Carrick Castle

> "Breaker, Breaker. Come in, Knockagh Monument. Can you hear me? This is Billy trying to reach you. I've cycled up to you and have shouted and waved to my ma from up there although she never responds, so she doesn't. We usually have my da's binoculars with us and can see everything down below, including Carrickfergus Castle and the Light House, so we can. Breaker, Breaker."

It was Joseph who had told Billy that the large structure which was near Carrick Castle was a lighthouse. He would go on to learn that it was actually the Kilroot Power Station which was a mile down the road from Carrick. It could be seen clearly from the Knockagh Monument.

By this time, he had been passed by several cars, some of which had their windows open with several kids in the back seat. Those same cars were now stopped at the traffic lights ahead of him. As Billy pulled up to the lights, he could hear them

# The Adventures of Silly Billy

saying that they did not think he was right in the head since he was talking into his fist and communicating with the Knockagh Monument.

Billy paid no attention. As he would go on to find, this helped him in passing the time as he got into a better rhythm and continued cycling. He was not doing any harm and in no time at all, had caught up to the other riders who were waiting for him just outside of the Green Island Golf Club. The group decided that they would forego taking the Station Road and would instead continue along Trooperslane Road.

Joseph pulled up alongside of Billy on his red Raleigh Chopper which he did not know that his brother had secretly named Lightning. He began cautioning him on the possible dangers that lay ahead.

> "Right, wee lad. Are you listening? Since you're so slow and are behind the group, my mates and I have already all talked about this, so we have. Now you need to know this.

# Silly Billy and the Escape from Carrick Castle

Once we get over there and part way down Trooperslane, we are going to come across train tracks. Make sure that you are paying full attention and look for the level crossing that will be flashing, as well as the bell that sounds to warn if a train is coming. The gate there will swing closed to stop cars. Do not try and cross unless you know it is completely safe. D'you hear me?"

Billy nodded in agreement. He knew exactly what his brother was referring to since they would often come across trains while going to pick up their dad, Charles, who would sometimes fly home instead of coming into Larne on the Sealink Ferry. On the times that they made the journey towards the Aldergrove airport, they had to cross one level crossing. Their mum, Catherine, was always very cautious when approaching this, which would allow Billy and his siblings to look both ways up and down the railway tracks to see if a train was coming. For whatever reason though, and

# The Adventures of Silly Billy

although the lights, bells, and the swinging gate at the level crossing were there to protect them all, Billy was always scared of it and would stare, telling himself that everything would be alright. He thought that the two lights on the top of the level crossing were like red eyes that were watching him, and that the amber light was its mouth.

As they made their way on down the Old Carrick Road which had now changed its name to the Upper Road, they finally reached their point and turned right onto the Trooperslane Road. As they approached the level crossing, there were no bells or red lights flashing. The gates on both sides of the road were closed. Even though Billy knew it was safe, he kept both of his hands on the handlebars and pedalled quickly. He stared at the lights to make sure that they didn't turn on suddenly or start staring at him with their red eyes and amber mouth.

While he continued to pedal and since his father had taken him to all the Star Wars

# Silly Billy and the Escape from Carrick Castle

movies, he thought that perhaps if he tried staring at something with a full, determined focus and concentrating, this would provide him with Jedi mind power, and that he could control the lights at the level crossing. In this instance, it seemed to work.

Continuing along, Billy was happy to learn that everything from this point forward towards the Belfast Road was downhill. He wouldn't have to pedal in any gear, or worry about climbing the steep hill of this road. Billy, however, did not realize that he would have to do this on his way back after they were all done fishing.

Delighted that he had now reached the bottom and that some of the other riders had already taken the left turn towards the Carrickfergus Castle, Billy looked and was quite disappointed that there was still a lot of road to navigate before they would finally reach their destination. He decided to focus on the castle itself and the fact that he would be fishing again, just like he loved to do with his favourite uncle,

# The Adventures of Silly Billy

Malcolm, who would not call him 'Silly Billy' or his given name of Gregory, but instead referred to him as 'Gregorious'.

What seemed to be an eternity eventually came to pass as the castle grew closer and closer into sight. A was the case with the Knockagh Monument, the closer he got, the bigger it became. Yet when Billy was last up on the mountain and looked over towards Carrick, the castle looked so tiny. This was not the case at all.

Crossing the road and finally reaching the pathway that would take them to the top of the marina, Billy stopped to look at Carrickfergus and spoke about how much fun it would be to spend the day inside there instead. Each fellow remarked on how they had all done the same thing as Billy, and had gone to visit the castle with their school mates while under the watchful eyes of teachers. If only they had the money to pay their way in, they would have all gone up here instead and checked out this mighty, Norman structure which was still

## Silly Billy and the Escape from Carrick Castle

very much intact compared to many of the other castles around Ireland that were now in ruins, including the Dunluce Castle which was located not far from the Giants Causeway on the North Antrim Coast.

Although they all stopped to catch their breaths from cycling seven miles and while staring at the sloping pathway that led up into the castle, Billy remembered that his mum had told him there was a famous song about Carrickfergus. Being his usual cheeky self, Billy reworked the lyrics and the music for 'The Belle of Belfast City:'

> "I'll tell me ma, when I get home, Carrickfergus Castle was built by a gnome. We took our bikes, we pedalled there, auld King Billy has a statue there. He's not handsome, he's not pretty, I'm sure he's not from Belfast City. Seagulls poo on his frizzy hair; that's dead on, it's better up there."

Laughing, but shaking his head at the same time, Joseph looked at his brother and said, "Ack. Would you quit acting the eejit and come on. Everyone wants to get fishing already, so they do."

The bikes were all discarded along the marina wall and fishing rods were set. Billy asked his brother and the others to put the wiggly worms onto his hooks since he hated the feeling of them squirming in his hands while he tried to do so.

Once he was set and remembering how he was taught by his uncle on how to set the reel, he casted his line into Belfast Lough, waited for his first bite, and hoped to catch the biggest fish although he did not have any bionic arms to reel it in.

After a while, they were becoming bored since they were catching crabs and slimy eels that were considered to be a delicacy from the loughs in and around Northern Ireland. Joseph whispered to his brother and asked if he wanted to head into the castle with him to check it out without having any school teachers shouting at them for not listening.

# Silly Billy and the Escape from Carrick Castle

"Sure, don't we need money? They won't let us in, so they won't," replied Billy.

"As a matter of fact," said Joseph. "I have a few pounds on me and could get the two of us in. Would you believe Da left his money lying around? I thought that we could use some of it. Sure, he won't even notice that it is missing, so he won't."

As Joseph watched, Billy's eyes grew wider. "But, that's stealing, so it is. You're going to get us into trouble, so you are. If da finds out that you took his money, he's going be mad and will send us to our rooms for hours. We'll never get to go fishing ever again, so we won't."

"Shh," came the reply. "Would you be quiet before you get us both in trouble," said Joseph. "I'm telling you right now that as long as you keep quiet about it, Da will never know. If he asks about it, just say that you were outside playing and went fishing."

Reluctantly, yet along with his older brother who he looked up too, Billy left his

# The Adventures of Silly Billy

fishing rod with their mates. They cycled back along the marina, up the ramp of the castle, and eventually under the portcullis before parking their matching Raleigh Choppers by the front entrance. While Joseph paid their way in, Billy stayed back and carefully read the instructions that were on a small wooden table. Eventually, Joseph came back out. He and Billy went to explore the historic walls of the keep without the watchful eyes of any teachers.

After taking in several of the attractions, and at one point, Billy and Joseph somehow ended up in one of the lower dungeon areas. The only problem is that these were completely off limits to ALL guests of the castle. They looked out towards the end of the marina at their mates, who were still trying to catch something. It seemed one lad was super excited and had caught a fish. It turned out to be an old welly boot.

From here, Joseph was able to call out to his mates through the grates which barred

# Silly Billy and the Escape from Carrick Castle

the narrow slots that acted as windows. Two of them came over to see what Billy and Joseph were doing. Joseph asked if they would like to come in to join him and Billy, and that the four of them could have fun touring and running around the castle. The friends asked how as they didn't have any tickets.

Joseph looked at Billy and asked said, "Give me your ticket. Hurry up, will ye."

Before Billy could argue, Joseph decided to give his mates both of their tickets. He then instructed them that if they were stopped at the entrance, they were to say that they had bought them earlier that day and wanted to come in for another look around.

Billy looked at Joseph and said, "No. This isn't a good idea. I don't want to get into any troub..."

Billy's words were cut off by his older brother who then said, "Right. Whatever you do, you DO NOT mention our names or

# The Adventures of Silly Billy

that you got these from us. Got it? Dead on. See you soon. C'mon in. We'll wait for you inside the castle, so we will."

What Joseph thought was great in planning, was definitely not great in its execution. When their mates got to the entrance and presented their tickets, something had already gone horribly wrong...

Joseph and Billy continued to run about the castle, checking out the various coats of arms, the knights' chainmail, and the armour that had been used so many centuries before. Their hope was to brag to their mates what they would be looking at even though they had already saw the items before on their own school trips.

They were about to make their way down to the lower level to meet up with their mates, but were suddenly stopped in their tracks. Joseph put his hand to Billy's mouth who was now nervously asking questions under hushed tones as to try and not be heard.

# Silly Billy and the Escape from Carrick Castle

"Shh. Be quiet. Don't say one word. Listen up."

Following his brother's instructions and while holding his breath to ensure that he would not be heard, Billy listened carefully as a set of high heels went loudly clicking across the castle floor, along with two very authoritative voices who were announcing that they were looking for two boys that had come in to the castle earlier, Joseph and Gregory. Obviously, they knew exactly who to look for, as they also knew their first names and had full descriptions of what they were wearing that day.

Joseph asked Billy what went wrong who in turn tried to remind him that he did not think it was a good idea in the first place and that they would most likely get into trouble, but that his brother wouldn't hear it. The plan that seemed so perfect must have been filled with holes.

Billy started asking Joseph several questions about their friends. However, Joseph was too busy trying to devise an

## The Adventures of Silly Billy

escape plan, looking at the map that had been provided to them so that they could get out.

Billy was fearful, as he had read about what happened to people who were captured trying to break into the castle. Was it possible that their friends who wanted to have a day of fishing beside Carrickfergus had instead been interrogated, undergone a tar and feathering, were tortured some more, and were then impaled within the confines of an Iron Maiden if they did not give up Billy and his brother? Perhaps they would be the first ones to find out that the fish which had been caught within the Belfast Lough would now instead be falling through the hole above the portcullis, and that they would be forced to eat their guts, scales, and fish bones as their punishment for invading the castle in the first place. Billy was obviously extremely nervous at the thought of this happening.

Looking at Billy, Joseph said that he had a plan.

# Silly Billy and the Escape from Carrick Castle

"Listen carefully. Just like in the movies, we have spent many hours each night, after dark, practicing our escape from difficult places and being chased by others by climbing over walls, hiding behind bushes, and using our cat-walk techniques."

Nervously, Billy nodded in full agreement. He knew exactly what his brother was referring to. Now was the time to make a quick getaway. There was no time like the present to put those plans and efforts into full action. Billy was more afraid of what his father and mother was going to do to them if they were to find out about their daring escape.

Since Billy and Joseph had decided to wear their soft-soled guddies before they left the house, they had a bit of an advantage over the staff since they could not detect them scurrying like two church mice across the floors of the castle. Billy did not realise that he could run so well while on his tiptoes, and felt the air whisking through his hair.

# The Adventures of Silly Billy

Billy followed Joseph, who had bolted in one direction to take an extremely worn, stone staircase back down to the lower level of the castle, as they had only just come up that way in an attempt to escape the staff that had been looking for them. Everything seemed to be going good since they had not been spotted thus far. However, that was until they hit the top step and began their descent down the spiral staircase within one of the towers.

"They might have come up this way," said one of the two staff members who were looking for them. The clicking sound of the high heels now started ascending towards them.

Since the exit was blocked, Joseph turned and came straight back up the three stairs that he and Billy were about to go down, their voices in hushed tones. Joseph grabbed Billy by the arm, now taking him on a full sprint from within this mighty structure and out to the outside walls. This is where archers, with arrow heads dipped

# Silly Billy and the Escape from Carrick Castle

in tar and were then set on fire, would have stood so many centuries before to protect the castle from encroaching ships. This time, however, it was the staff who were protecting the castle from Billy, his brother, and his mates from the Knockview and Woodford areas of Newtownabbey.

This was an upper wall. The problem was that Billy and Joseph had no way down except for them to both jump separately into the grassy courtyard below. It was certainly not an immediate option for either one of them, but they had no other choice at this point.

Being the braver of two, Joseph wasted no time. While keeping his head low, he instructed Billy to do the same as they snuck along the wall and down to where Thunder and Lightning, their getaway matching Raleigh Choppers, were waiting for them in the exact same spot that they had left them. They had always been very careful to ensure that they locked their bikes up. For whatever reason, however,

## The Adventures of Silly Billy

they did not do so on this one occasion, which would aid them in their terrifying escape from the staff that were now in full pursuit of them.

Joseph lowered himself to his knees and hung unto the edge of the wall before sliding his legs over, and dropped to the lawn area below. Billy hesitated only to be prompted by him and his panicked voice.

"C'mon. Hurry up, will ye? Let's go. There's no time to waste, so there's not. Get a move on."

In a panic and not thinking that he could do it, Billy immediately took the same leap of faith below with a dead thud. The fall winded him, but with the adrenaline surge pumping through his body, he didn't have time to think about it. He wanted to get away like there was no tomorrow, which would be the case if he ended up in an Iron Maiden.

Billy thought that there must have been smoke billowing from the chains on their

# Silly Billy and the Escape from Carrick Castle

bikes and tyres as he and his brother pedalled down the ramp as fast and as furious as their legs would allow them. He refused to look back to see if any of the staff had maybe found a bicycle that did not have a lock on the wheel and would try to follow them to the end of the marina. Directly in front of them was the Belfast Lough, boats, wiggly worms, crusty crabs with big claws, slimy eels, and their fishing rods. There was no other escape route.

As they pedalled and with his imagination being as active as it was, more so now that he was seeking his freedom, Billy wondered if the staff who were in pursuit of him and his brother had come up with another plan to capture them. Perhaps they had decided to unglue the cannon balls from the ground, load them into the cannons around the walls, point them towards the marina, and would take aim at their bicycles. This would ensure that Billy, his brother, and their mates who were still fishing, could not escape and would instead be held captive in the dungeon with their

## The Adventures of Silly Billy

two friends who had tried to storm the castle with their free tickets.

That thought was immediately replaced by another. Billy wondered if the staff member with the high heels that had clicked so loudly across the floor of the castle would now be walking towards the marina. Would she be wearing the knights' chainmail and armour that was used centuries before? And, after capturing and rather than torture them with fish bones and scales, she would tie him, his brother, his mates, and the two prisoners to the King Billy statue so that the seagulls could teach them a lesson and poo on them all together. He put Thunder into third gear and pedalled like he had never done before.

Billy and his brother arrived back at the safety of the marina, out of breath, and where Joseph's mates stood with stunned looks on their faces. Obviously, they had lived to tell a tale of how they themselves escaped, and did not become permanent fixtures within the dungeon walls. Their

# Silly Billy and the Escape from Carrick Castle

two friends who had been caught by the staff were also standing there, neither one of them had been tarred, feathered, or tortured within the wooden stocks at the front entrance of the castle. Nor did it look like they had fish slop dropped onto them from above the portcullis.

Billy was quite surprised by this, but was still worried that the staff were going to come after them. Some seagulls were flying around, while others seemed to be trying to get close to the worms that were sitting on the marina since everyone was so distracted at their arrival. Billy clapped his hands loudly to try and shoo them away.

With his hands on his knees, out of breath and panting heavily while talking between gasps, Billy said that he would never go back after this terrifying escape from Carrickfergus Castle. It would be the last time that he would ever step foot into this mighty Norman structure.

Along with his mates, his brother decided that they also did not want to be

# The Adventures of Silly Billy

down by the marina either in case the staff did indeed came looking for them there. They all had more than enough adventures for one day, and agreed that it would be best if no one spoke to their parents about what had happened after their extremely close call.

As the others started to reel in their lines and dismantled their fishing rods, Billy decided that he would make one more cast before calling it a day. It wasn't even a minute later when Billy felt his rod make that huge tugging feeling, the one that he had felt before while out fishing with his uncle at the Boghill dam. He knew that a massive fish, which was more than likely the biggest fish of the day, was at the end of his line and was telling him that it was waiting to be caught. Billy held his rod and did not move. If only he had not had gone in to the castle with his brother, he would have had quite the story to tell.

When the line stopped tugging, Billy decided to reel it in. There was no wiggly

# Silly Billy and the Escape from Carrick Castle

worm on the hook anymore. Instead, it was clean. Hanging his head, he dismantled his rod and decided to make the long trip back with the other lads to their homes on their bicycles. Billy knew that going up the Trooperslane Road this time was going to be so much more difficult than it was coming down it. Sure enough, the ride back seemed to take forever. Billy thought that they were never going to make it home after all, and that he would never see the bicycle tracks at the bottom of his street again either.

When the group finally reached Knockview and Woodford, they all went their separate ways. Billy and Joseph returned to their home, put their fishing rods away in the garage, and walked into the house only to be met by their father who was staring at them with a puzzled look.

"Gregory. Joseph. How was your day?" he bellowed.

It was not often that their father called him by his nickname, Silly Billy. Since he

# The Adventures of Silly Billy

was always away at sea, it was very rare that Charles ever got a chance to see a lot of the silly things that Billy did, although he often read about them in the letters that their mother, Catherine, would send off to him each month. Charles continued from where he had left of.

"What did you boys do today?", he enquired. After casting a knowing look directly at Billy, it was Joseph who decided to respond.

"Ah. Nothing much. I got some worms from ma's rose bushes outside and we went fishing with my mates. We caught crabs, eels, a stingray flatfish, and a welly boot. We put everything back into the ocean. Except for the boot, of course."

His dad asked his next question which they both wished he wouldn't.

"Fishing? Oh, okay. Did you happen to see some money that I left on the table? I am sure that there was quite a few more pounds here than what there is now."

# Silly Billy and the Escape from Carrick Castle

Billy looked at Joseph. He did not want to get either himself or his brother into more trouble. He knew full well that it was his brother who had helped himself to a few pounds. He also knew that his brother had used that money to bring them into the castle before the two of them handed over their tickets to their mates. He knew that their friends had been caught and had to tell the staff where they got the tickets from, and that they had to make a daring escape from the castle and would never go back ever again. Before they could speak though, their father continued.

"Ack, sure, it does not matter. It's okay. C'mon, you boys, the car is waiting for us. Time to go."

While sitting together in the back seat in silence, which was quite rare for them to do, the family car rumbled along Knockview Park, down Knockview Road, left onto the Doagh Road and then turned right along the Old Carrick Road past their forested playground. His dad would often take them

# The Adventures of Silly Billy

into Belfast to see movies such as Star Wars, The Black Hole, James Bond, along with all of the new Disney movies including the ones about a car named Herby. Billy figured that this was perhaps the reason for the sudden surprise.

It was Billy who finally asked their father where they were going.

"So, da," said Billy. "Whereabouts are we off too today? A film at the ABC theatre? Or are we going to the Curzon like we always do?"

"Well," said Charles. "I wanted to give you boys a wee surprise. Your mummy is out in Belfast with your two sisters visiting your granny. And since the latest Star Trek movie finally made it to Northern Ireland, I thought that I had enough money for us to have popcorn, drinks, and an ice cream. I know those are your favourite sweets but since there is not enough money, we will have to go another day with your sisters."

"I see," said Billy with a huge sigh as he glanced towards his brother.

# Silly Billy and the Escape from Carrick Castle

Making sure that it was safe and that he wouldn't be seen, Billy quietly mouthed, "You shouldn't have taken that money, so you shouldn't."

"It's alright, boys," said their father. "I know that you are both quite disappointed, so I thought that we could do something else instead that doesn't cost as much and that we could all go together. It will be a lot of fun, I promise."

"Oh?" said Billy excitedly. "Where are we going instead?"

His father responded. "I don't think that you've ever been before or have ever seen what it has to offer. I used to go there as a child with my schoolmates. I usually depart from Larne and never get a chance to see it, but when I go sailing after launching from Belfast, it brings me back to my childhood days. I thought that we could all create our own wonderful memories and go on a wee visit to a very special place... Carrickfergus Castle!"

# The Adventures of Silly Billy

Escaping from Carrickfergus Castle was quite a scary adventure. In fact, I did not return there for twenty-six years since that adventure occurred! I often wondered if the staff there would still be looking for bossy boots and I if we were ever to step foot back onto the grounds of this mighty Norman structure built in 1177 on the shores of Belfast Lough.

I guess what is just as scary, is that we ended up moving a year or so after that adventure had occurred. And where did we move too? The place that has the vampire flies called mosquitoes, who buzz all around Winnipeg, Canada. Yes, they do indeed bite people and suck their blood but thankfully, they do not like the cold weather. Although sometimes there is no school because of all the snow and that kids do enjoy their snow days, we still have pesky vampire flies also known as mosquitoes!

# Silly Billy and the Escape from Carrick Castle

Sadly, this brings Volume 1 of my ~~Trilogy~~ ~~Trillogy~~ Sillogy to an end. I hope that you enjoyed my childhood stories so far, so I do! Keep your eyes peeled though, as I am currently writing the second volume in The Adventures of Silly Billy! And just so you know, the first story of the second book will be called:

Silly Billy and the Donegal Voyage...

THE END, SO IT IS!

# The Adventures of Silly Billy

## Student Reviews for The Adventures of Silly Billy

**Gr. 10 Students from:**
**Mr. Mauricio Barra – Teacher**
**Daniel McIntyre Collegiate Institute**

*"As a young girl who has not lived all her life in Winnipeg, similarly to the author, I can relate immensely to the childhood McVicker details in The Adventures of Silly Billy. In his writings, he perfectly encapsulates all that childhood is; the innocence of the matter and the countless blunders which follow close behind. What I find truly admirable about McVicker's style, though, is his ability to make of his childhood a comedic story as well as a tale of warning."*

- Riham Abdullah, (age 15),
Winnipeg, Manitoba, Canada.

*"So, first of all, I thank you for providing me this wonderful opportunity of being one of the first readers of your book. When I first saw the title I was totally intrigued as to what the story was going to be about, because after all, I wasn't familiar with what the term "silly billy" meant. The characters grew on me pretty fast, especially Billy since I can relate to him the most. Most of the events that happened throughout the story reminded me about all the funny little accidents I caused back then. Although I*

# The Adventures of Silly Billy

*am pretty sure that I'm not as clumsy as Billy, I did recall ripping my new gown the very first time I put it on, which was on my birthday.*

*Your book made me laugh a whole lot! It was a very fresh kind of story to me actually, mostly because I rarely read stories that are based on true events, and I really love it! I would have wished for a longer one though, since the theme and characters of the book already grew on me even for a short period of time. It's a book full of adventures everybody can relate to! And I'm not afraid to admit that I can relate very well to it. Have a nice day!"*

- Anastacia Hernandez (age 15),<br>Winnipeg, Manitoba, Canada.


*"The Adventures of Silly Billy is the best book I have ever read. It is not just a book full of adventures, but a book full of interesting ideas. In reading this book, I learned that it is necessary to follow instructions and not use shortcuts since they are often wrong cuts. I find this book compelling and fun to read."*

- Bana Ataklti (age 15),<br>Winnipeg, Manitoba, Canada.

# The Adventures of Silly Billy

## Acknowledgements

To my beloved sister, Karen McVicker, an inspirational woman who did not know the meaning of the word 'quit.' I watched as you waged a courageous fight; a monumental battle against Acute Lymphoblastic Leukemia over four years. Your fierce determination was beyond measure. Although my world changed when your battle finally came to an end, I can only hope to have simply but an ounce of your strength if I am ever faced with a tremendous challenge such as the one you tackled head first. I love and miss you. Rest peacefully, sis, for you have certainly earned the right do so.

– **Karen Theresa McVicker.**
  **May 17, 1967 – November 8, 2015.**


To my wonderful kids: my daughter, Caitlin McVicker, and my son, Ciarán McVicker. Words can never truly express this, but you are my special gifts in this journey called life. You create infinite memories for me, for which I cannot count my blessings enough. In the words of the brilliant children's author, Robert Munch:

*I love you for always,*
*I love you forever.*
*As long as I'm living,*
*My babies you'll be.*

# The Adventures of Silly Billy

The Adventures of Silly Billy are based on the true-life childhood experiences and memories of Irish Author, Poet, and Storyteller, Greg McVicker, while he was growing up just on the outskirts of Belfast, Northern Ireland.

Every character within this book are Greg's family, friends, and people that he knew within his community of Newtownabbey, County Antrim. The street names are all real. The main character – Silly Billy – is fully based upon Greg himself.

Although personal dedications to several, incredibly wonderful people lie within the pages of this book and who made my memories of yesteryear as special as they were, I would also like to acknowledge some of the individuals who are within these stories.

Each of them were very much a part of my family, my friends, and my community. Without them all, my childhood could have both looked and been extremely different. Unfortunately, that did indeed eventually become the case with all the sectarian hatred, bitterness, and cancerous targeting of innocent people and families who lived in and around my neighbourhood, including some who lived within our circles. However, many of you helped in shaping my earlier days and for which I am eternally grateful.

# The Adventures of Silly Billy

While some have since passed and never had the chance to see these wee stories and reminders from our forgotten days of a much happier time, I would like to express my deepest thanks to:

My mum, Catherine, my dad, Charles, and my siblings, Karen, Joseph, and Angela;

Mr. and Mrs. Andrew and Anne McComish, and their son, Iain;

Mr. and Mrs. Roy and May Noble;

Mr. and Mrs. Dennis and Mary Maher;

Mr. and Mrs. Harry and Penny Scott;

My childhood mates and quite literally, my second family: Denis, John, and Rosemary Maher, as well as Richard Rainey;

To Kristine, Linda, Zoe, Scarlet, Dale, Lauren, Shannon, Sam, Ethan, Jen, Jean, Christopher, Michelle, Gráinne, Riham, Anastacia, Bana, and Katelyn, thank you all so very much for taking the time to read the manuscript in advance and provide your amazing thoughts and feedback! I am extremely humbled, and truly appreciate each and every one of them.

And to countless more people although there are far too many to name… cheers!

# The Adventures of Silly Billy

## Other Titles from Greg McVicker

**Through the Eyes of a Belfast Child:**
*Life. Personal Reflections. Poems.*

**First Edition** - May 2014
**Second Edition** - November 2017

*"This is totally fantastic! Even the wee poems were such a pleasure to read. This is something I'd read again and again. Above all, I'm sure your mammy is looking down on you with such pride and love. I have never read such beautiful words written by anyone to describe their mum as you have. The feelings are there, but putting them into words is something else. I actually filled up reading some parts, a wee mixture of smiles and tears. I'm sure that anyone else who reads this will react exactly the same. Not only have you put a lot of hard work and time into this, you've also written this with your heart."*

- Teresa McAuley.
Belfast, County Antrim, Northern Ireland.

**ISBN:** 978-1-7751622-8-5 (Hardcover)
978-1-7751622-6-1 (Softcover)
978-1-7751622-7-8 (eBook)

# The Adventures of Silly Billy

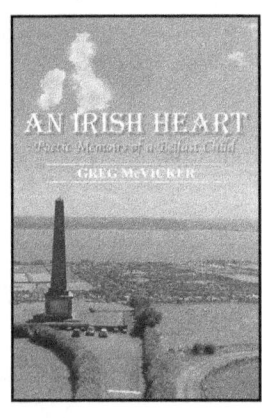

**An Irish Heart:**
*Poetic Memoirs of a Belfast Child*

**First Edition**  – October 23, 2017

*"The Book and Poetry are so special. It is a very heartwarming, disturbing, and complex view of how things were from Greg's journey from his beloved 'Norn Iron' to Canada, and beyond, with great principles at work in himself, and from many others whom he met along the way. It incorporates Spiritual, Psychological, and Political Dimensions. Greg's journey proves again, that despite cruelty, and terrible conditions, human beings can somehow get through the worst that life throws at us, with love, support, and friendship, which re-ignites 'the Will to Live'. His Irish, Canadian, and Humanitarian Spirit looms large through his writing and his beautiful poetry. It is profound, funny, and moving. It deserves to be read carefully to the end, in a spirit of meditative reflection in order to fully appreciate the character of the man and his journey."*

- Gerry Rogers.
Edinburgh, Scotland.

**ISBN:** 978-1-7751622-1-6 (eBook)
978-1-7751622-0-9 (Softcover)

# The Adventures of Silly Billy

**One Cross to Bear:**
*Humanity Through Narrative Prose*

**First Edition — October 23, 2017**

*"Using his distinctive style of storytelling by way of stanza and prose, Irish Poet and Author, Greg McVicker, dives headfirst into the turbulent cycle of life. In "One Cross to Bear", his latest collection of poetry, he takes us on a whirlwind journey of his years growing up in his native Northern Ireland, up to the present day in Canada. Poems such as; "Belfast City Asylum" and "Everlasting Homesickness" paint a vivid picture of growing up in war-torn Belfast, and the pain he endured at being torn away from all that he knew in order to start a new life in a safer, but foreign land. Greg writes unashamedly from the heart, reaching out to his readers and carrying them along the waves of an emotional tsunami. I have no doubt that these poetic stories have and will continue to affect untold numbers of individuals throughout their lifetime."*

- J.P. Sexton,
Author of; 'The Big Yank – Memoir of a Boy Growing Up Irish.'

**ISBN:** 978-1-7751622-3-0 (eBook)
978-1-7751622-2-3 (Softcover)

# The Adventures of Silly Billy

**The Adventures of Silly Billy:**
*Silly Billy and the Postage Stamp*

**First Edition**     – January 14, 2015 (eBook)

**Second Edition** – May 3, 2016 (Softcover)

**Third Edition**   – November 2017

**Silly Billy and the Postage Stamp:**

*In this first adventure, and since his father is away at sea, Billy wants to be like his older brother who assumes the role of being the "Man of the House", and bosses his siblings around. Given a simple task of posting a letter to their father, this comical true-life story which is set in the community of Newtownabbey, Northern Ireland, captures the childhood experiences of Irish Author and Poet, Greg McVicker, in how one young boy can take a simple task and make a complete mess of it. The moral of this story is to not try covering up ones' countless mistakes and mishaps along the way as eventually they will be found out.*

**ISBN:**         978-1-7751622-5-4 (eBook)
                    978-1-7751622-4-7 (Softcover)

# The Adventures of Silly Billy

**The Adventures of Silly Billy: Silly Billy and the Good Deed**

**First Edition** – May 17, 2016 (Softcover)
**Second Edition** – November 2017

**Silly Billy and the Good Deed:**

*In this second adventure, and since the tuck shop at his primary school is all sold out, Billy is asked to help his teacher get her favourite sweets along with his own reward. However, what should have taken only a few moments becomes an amusing escapade that is filled with numerous misfortunes due to Billy not following very specific directions. This hilarious true-life story which takes place in Newtownabbey, Northern Ireland, captures the childhood experiences of Irish Author and Poet, Greg McVicker, and his memories from years gone by. The moral of this story is to try your best, but to also do as one is told to do in the first place.*

**ISBN:** 978-1-7751622-5-4 (eBook)
978-1-7751622-4-7 (Softcover)

# The Adventures of Silly Billy

**The Adventures of Silly Billy:**
*Silly Billy and the
Escape from Carrick Castle*

**First Edition     – November 2017**

**Silly Billy and the
Escape from Carrick Castle:**

*In this third adventure, Billy is offered a chance to go fishing with his older brother and his mates alongside of the marina beside a Norman castle built in 1177 on the northern shores of Belfast Lough in Carrickfergus. Once there, however, fishing seems to be the last thing on their minds and leads to a troublesome chase within the confines of this mighty structure. This hysterical true-life reflection which took place in Newtownabbey, Northern Ireland, captures the childhood experiences of Irish Author and Poet, Greg McVicker. The moral of this story is that your freedom might not quite be your fate, especially when your father comes home.*

**ISBN:**          978-1-7751622-5-4 (eBook)
               978-1-7751622-4-7 (Softcover)

# The Adventures of Silly Billy

## Connect with the Author

I would love to hear your story, for who knows what kind of higher learning or healing can come from it, or how it can help support someone else by knowing that they are not alone in their journey of life.

If you are interested in connecting with me, please feel free to do so. I make every effort to respond to all enquiries within a timely manner, and certainly look forwards to hearing from you!

| | |
|---|---|
| **facebook:** | ThroughtheEyesofaBelfastChild |
| **email:** | gmcvicker70@gmail.com |
| **twitter:** | @BelfastChild70 |
| **hashtag:** | #BelfastChild |

www.ingramcontent.com/pod-product-compliance
Lightning Source LLC
Chambersburg PA
CBHW071844080526
44589CB00012B/1110